Trail and
Fell Running
in the Lake District

40 runs in
the National
Park including
classic race routes

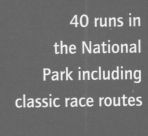

About the Author

Kingsley Jones lives in Ambleside in the Lake District, and also spends part of the year in the Alps. His peripatetic lifestyle enables him to guide running groups in the mountains throughout the year, and his qualifications range from UIMLA International Mountain Leader to Personal Trainer.

Over the years Kingsley has participated in many mountain running events, both in the UK and internationally. Highlights include the Tor des Géants (Italy), five Ultra Trail du Mont Blanc (UTMB) series finishes, Zermatt Marathon, Lakes in a Day, Tour of Helvellyn, and countless others.

In the same series as this book, Kingsley also wrote the Cicerone guidebook *Trail Running – Chamonix and the Mont Blanc region*, which details 40 routes in the Chamonix Valley, Italy and Switzerland. He runs a mountain running and guiding company (www.icicle.co.uk), which has an outdoor and runners shop in Windermere. While researching all the routes in this book, Kingsley was accompanied by Maximus, his ever-faithful four-legged training partner.

Twitter: @KingsleyJones
Website: www.kingsleyjones.com

Trail and
Fell Running

in the Lake District

**40 runs
in the National Park
including classic race routes**

by Kingsley Jones

2 Police Square, Milnthorpe
Cumbria LA7 7PY

www.cicerone.co.uk

© Kingsley Jones 2017
First edition 2017
ISBN-13: 978 1 85284 880 4

Printed in China on behalf of
Latitude Press Ltd

A catalogue record for this book is
available from the British Library.

Route mapping
by Lovell Johns
www.lovelljohns.com

All photographs are by the author
unless otherwise stated.

© Crown copyright 2017
OS PU100012932.
NASA relief data courtesy of ESRI

Updates to this guide

While every effort is made by our authors
to ensure the accuracy of guidebooks
as they go to print, changes can occur
during the lifetime of an edition. Any
updates that we know of for this guide
will be on the Cicerone website (www.
cicerone.co.uk/880/updates), so please
check before planning your trip. We
also advise that you check information
about such things as transport,
accommodation and shops locally. Even
rights of way can be altered over time.

We are always grateful for information
about any discrepancies between
a guidebook and the facts on the
ground, sent by email to updates@
cicerone.co.uk or by post to

Cicerone
2 Police Square
Milnthorpe LA7 7PY
United Kingdom.

*Front cover: Fell running near Lang How, with
the backdrop of the Langdale Pikes (Route 7)*

*This book is dedicated to my daughter
Freya, a real mountain girl, who started
fell running aged 3. Run with the wind.*

Acknowledgements

This book is the result of a lifetime of
discovering and running in the Lake
District, and countless pairs of worn-out
fell running shoes. There are too many
people to thank for their input, but I'm
deeply indebted to all the running clients
and friends who accompanied me on
the routes, and none more so than my
Bernese mountain dog Maximus, who
knows these routes better than anyone
else. Thank you all for running with
me on the good days, and the others
of wind, snow, ice, floods and rain!

A huge thanks to all the team at Cicerone
for their support and belief in this project:
Jonathan, Joe and Andrea, and also to
Georgia for her patience in editing. This
book is my second in their new running
series, and I'm eternally grateful to
Cicerone for listening to this idea.

My biggest debt of gratitude is to
my wife Sarah for putting up with me
doing endless route research, which
anyone less charitable might have
described as escaping the house
to go on yet another fell run!

Contents

Features on the overview map

——— County/Unitary boundary

     Urban area

     National Park
eg **LAKE DISTRICT**

     Area of Outstanding
Natural Beauty
eg *Arnside & Silverdale AONB*

Route symbols on OS map extracts
(for OS legend see printed OS maps)

     route

     alternative route

(SF) start/finish point

     route direction

0   1km

0   0.5 mile

The extracts from 1:50,000 OS maps
used in this book have been reproduced
at 1:40,000 for greater clarity

GPX files

GPX files for all routes can be downloaded free at www.cicerone.co.uk/880/GPX.

Grisedale Tarn in the late afternoon light (Route 39)

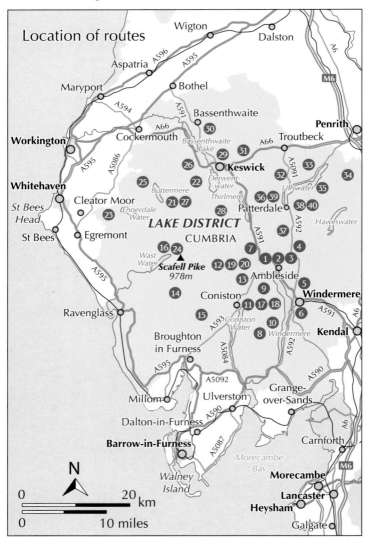

Location of routes

8

Route summary table

No.	Name	Start/Finish	Distance	Ascent/Descent	Grade	Time	Page
1	Loughrigg Fell circuit	Royal Oak, Ambleside	9.8km (6 miles)	410m (1345ft)	Trail run, Level 2	1hr 40min	39
2	Wansfell and Troutbeck	White Lion, Ambleside	9.8km (6 miles)	475m (1560ft)	Trail run, Level 2	1hr 45min	43
3	Fairfield Horseshoe	Golden Rule, Ambleside	19.7km (12¼ miles)	1120m (3675ft)	Fell run, Level 2	3hr 40min	46
4	Stony Cove circuit	Kirkstone Inn, Kirkstone Pass	10.6km (6½ miles)	540m (1770ft)	Fell run, Level 3	2hr	53
5	Kentmere skyline	Mortal Man, Troutbeck	29.2km (18 miles)	1365m (4480ft)	Fell run, Level 2	4hr 50min	57
6	Windermere and Kentmere	The Elleray, Windermere	19.7km (12¼ miles)	540m (1770ft)	Trail run, Level 1	3hr 5min	63
7	Easedale and Blea Rigg	Tweedies Bar, Grasmere	11.9km (7½ miles)	520m (1705ft)	Fell run, Level 2	2hr 10min	69
8	Grizedale Forest	Eagles Head, Satterthwaite	12.7km (8 miles)	340m (1115ft)	Trail run, Level 1	1hr 55min	73
9	Black Crag and Tarn Hows	Drunken Duck, Barngates	8.5km (5¼ miles)	265m (870ft)	Trail run, Level 2	1hr 20min	77
10	Claife Heights	Cuckoo Brow, Far Sawrey	15.3km (9½ miles)	365m (1200ft)	Trail run, Level 1	2hr 10min	80
11	Old Man of Coniston	Black Bull, Coniston	14.1km (8¾ miles)	945m (3100ft)	Fell run, Level 2	2hr 55min	86
12	Langdale Horseshoe	Old Dungeon Ghyll, Langdale	19.2km (12 miles)	1310m (4300ft)	Fell run, Level 4	3hr 50min	92
13	Three Shires loop	Three Shires Inn, Little Langdale	18.2km (11¼ miles)	1270m (4170ft)	Fell run, Level 3	3hr 35min	97

No.	Name	Start/Finish	Distance	Ascent/Descent	Grade	Time	Page
14	Boot and Scafell	Woolpack Inn, Hardknott	17.2km (10¾ miles)	910m (2990ft)	Fell run, Level 2	3hr 5min	101
15	Duddon Valley	Newfield Inn, Duddon Valley	9.8km (6 miles)	230m (755ft)	Trail run, Level 2	1hr 35min	107
16	Scafell Pike	Wasdale Head Inn, Wasdale	34.8km (21½ miles)	2450m (8040ft)	Fell run, Level 4	6hr 55min	110
17	Torver and Walna Scar	The Sun, Coniston	10.8km (6¾ miles)	280m (920ft)	Trail run, Level 1	1hr 45min	117
18	Coppermines Valley	Ship Inn, Coniston	13.4km (8¼ miles)	630m (2065ft)	Trail run, Level 3	2hr 25min	121
19	Langstrath loop	Sticklebarn pub, Langdale	19.4km (12 miles)	1040m (3410ft)	Fell run, Level 2	3hr 35min	124
20	Tilberthwaite loop	The Britannia pub, Elterwater	17.2km (10¾ miles)	485m (1590ft)	Trail run, Level 2	2hr 45min	129
21	Buttermere and High Stile	The Fish Inn, Buttermere	21.7km (13½ miles)	1590m (5220ft)	Fell run, Level 3	4hr 25min	134
22	Catbells and High Spy	Swinside Inn, Newlands	15.8km (9¾ miles)	685m (2250ft)	Fell run, Level 2	2hr 45min	139
23	Black Sail and Pillar	Fox and Hounds, Ennerdale Bridge	33.7km (20 miles)	1205m (3955ft)	Fell run, Level 3	5hr 25min	144
24	Kirk Fell tour	Wasdale Head Inn, Wasdale	8.7km (5½ miles)	580m (1905ft)	Fell run, Level 2	1hr 50min	151
25	Mellbreak and Crummock	Kirkstile Inn, Loweswater	9.7km (6 miles)	470m (1540ft)	Fell run, Level 3	1hr 45min	155
26	Coledale Horseshoe	Royal Oak, Braithwaite	13.8km (8½miles)	930m (3050ft)	Fell run, Level 3	2hr 45min	158
27	Buttermere Sailbeck loop	Bridge Hotel Inn, Buttermere	15.4km (9½ miles)	1135m (3725ft)	Fell run, Level 3	3hr 10min	162

No.	Name	Start/ Finish	Distance	Ascent/ Descent	Grade	Time	Page
28	Borrowdale loop	Scafell Hotel pub, Rosthwaite	26.5km (16½ miles)	1760m (5775ft)	Fell run, Level 4	5hr 5min	167
29	Walla Crag and Castlerigg	Dog & Gun pub, Keswick	10.6km (6½ miles)	300m (985ft)	Trail run, Level 1	1hr 40min	173
30	Skiddaw	The Sun Inn, Bassenthwaite	20.6km (12¾ miles)	1085m (3560ft)	Fell run, Level 3	3hr 50min	177
31	Blencathra loop	Horse & Farrier, Threlkeld	13.8km (8½ miles)	735m (2410ft)	Fell run, Level 4	2hr 30min	184
32	Dockray coach road	The Royal Hotel pub, Dockray	20.8km (13 miles)	795m (2610ft)	Fell run, Level 2	3hr 25min	188
33	Gowbarrow loop	Brackenrigg Inn, Watermillock	15.8km (9¾ miles)	525m (1720ft)	Trail run, Level 2	2hr 30min	193
34	Askham and Patterdale	Punchbowl Inn, Askham	33km (20½ miles)	760m (2495ft)	Trail run, Level 2	4hr 50min	198
35	Martindale circuit	Howtown Hotel, Howtown	18.5km (11½ miles)	825m (2705ft)	Fell run, Level 2	3hr 10min	204
36	Patterdale loop	Inn on the Lake, Glenridding	14.5km (9 miles)	190m (625ft)	Trail run, Level 1	2hr	209
37	High Street	Brotherswater Inn, Sykeside	20.9km (13 miles)	1200m (3940ft)	Fell run, Level 3	3hr 50min	213
38	Helvellyn skyline	White Lion Inn, Patterdale	14.6km (9 miles)	1025m (3365ft)	Fell run, Level 5	3hr 5min	219
39	Helvellyn tour	The Traveller's Rest, Glenridding	25.3km (15¾ miles)	1070m (3510ft)	Fell run, Level 2	4hr 10min	223
40	Pinnacle Ridge skyrunning	White Lion Inn, Patterdale	9.9km (6¼ miles)	705m (2315ft)	Sky run, Level 5	2hr	230

Runners on Route 13 navigating with a map

Introduction

This book will introduce you to the world of trail and fell running on some of the finest mountains of the world; the Lake District. They may not have the stark granite spires of the Mont Blanc massif, or the huge mountain faces of the Himalayas or the Andes, but the old weathered Cumbrian mountains exude a majesty and history that make them more quietly stunning and fascinating. It's a landscape that draws you in, with the next fell ever beckoning you to run its slopes, until the lure of a cosy pub beckons you back into the valley.

It was only at the end of writing this book that I realised what a personal journey it had been for me. I sat atop Jenkins Crag at sunset one glorious June evening, the surface of Windermere as still as a mirror below me, as the fells beyond caught the last rays of the sun; Wetherlam, Cold Pike, Crinkle Crags, Bowfell and Loughrigg. Each ridgeline, each crinkle, each notch on those fellsides was as familiar as my own hands, and a cascade of memories flooded in with each area my eyes focused on. To be lucky enough to live in the Lake District is one thing, but to feel so connected to these fells and to have learnt to read the running lines over them forges a permanent bond.

There is a rich history of mountain running in the UK, with the first recorded fell race in Braemar around 1040. The Lake District became the spiritual home to fell running, with the Guide's Race in each of the village fairs and sports days. These were first recorded in the 19th century, and one of the oldest events occurs each August in Grasmere. Keswick hotelier Bob Graham made a round of 42 fell tops within 24 hours in 1932, and this circuit has become a test piece for all fell runners.

Bob Graham took 23hr 39min, but the men's record now stands at 13hr 53min by Billy Bland in 1982, and the women's at 15hr 24min by Jasmin Paris in 2016. Joss Naylor ran an incredible round with 72 peaks in 23hr 20min in 1975. In 1970 the Fell Runners Association (FRA) was established, and there are now over 400 races each year in its calendar. Many records in fell running stand for an incredible length of time, such as Kenny Stuart's 18min 56sec record for the Wansfell race, set back in 1983.

Books have been written about the rich history of fell running, but there has been a growth in other facets of the sport of mountain running, including trail running and ultras. Some of this growth has been driven by the development of better clothing, equipment and training, but also changes in lifestyle and a challenge-based culture have seen a demand for the evolution of different styles of mountain running. Some runners want to stay on trails and paths, while others want to belt hell for leather over the open hillsides. What unites

Runners with Coniston Old Man behind (Route 11)

these various facets of the sport is that mountain running is driven by the simplicity and the joy of pushing one's limits in glorious scenery. Mountain running gives us freedom.

As humans we are born runners. Our Neolithic forefathers were persistence hunters, using a combination of running and tracking to pursue prey until it was exhausted. Nowadays we see the effects of modern diet and work environments having a detrimental impact on many people's health. The attraction of running is that it's a sport that comes naturally to us; it requires very little equipment, improves our health and has huge mental benefits too.

There's a natural progression for those who run to seek the next challenge – be it in terms of distance or on tougher terrain – and the mountains provide the most extreme medium in which to practise our sport. At the pinnacle of this, elite runners have run up famous mountains around the world including Mont Blanc, Kilimanjaro, Aconcagua and the Matterhorn at mind-boggling speeds.

One of the main draws of trail and fell running is that you move fast and unencumbered, in comparison to the average trekker or climber, and that opens up new horizons in what you can achieve. Mountain running brings a sense of liberation that it is rarely felt – even while walking or mountaineering.

Given the sport's increased popularity, gone are the preconceptions of mountain runners as wild mountain men with overly short shorts and wild beards. You're more likely to be overtaken by a woman in the latest technical compression fabrics with lightweight poles and a minimalist running backpack. Trail and fell running has come a long way in the last 20 years; it's more inclusive, more accessible, and more enjoyable than ever before.

In the Lake District, fell running is a way of life. The races are the beating heart of the sporting calendar in many of its villages. What still marks the region out is that despite its long history of running races, there's a great abiding amateur spirit. Many local fell races are organised by the local running club, with times written on stickers that are moved onto a board to record results. In these races there are no medals or race t-shirts, and no prize money either. Meanwhile, at the other end of the scale, there are big organised trail races such as the Lakeland 100 and Lakes in a Day, with all the glitz of a European event.

Fell running is more than the organised events though. It's a way of exploring the mountains, keeping fit, and spending time alone or with friends. Mountain running is far more than a selfish personal quest; it's a sport that brings people together, shares a love of the mountains, and inspires others. The aim of this book, and of the routes described, is to inspire you to enjoy this thrilling sport in one of its greatest playgrounds.

You are never too young or old to run

While goals such as pace, time and terrain will differ from runner to runner, the shared goal should be the pursuit of maximum enjoyment with the minimum of equipment or impact on the landscape.

This book is not a walking guidebook to the Lake District in the guise of a running guidebook. The routes selected are of specific interest to runners in terms of the terrain they cover, the distances travelled, or the vertical height gains encountered. Several routes adopt the course of some of the classic fell races, while others let you explore some of the quieter corners of the national park. Many of the lines that runners will take differ significantly from those taken by hillwalkers, and therefore use different landmarks and features. There's no rift between the runner and walker, but each politely think the other mad; runners don't understand how walkers can savour going so slow with their cumulative time on the legs, while walkers think the runners crazy for windmilling down slopes at breakneck speeds.

The intention is to share with the reader some of the best locations for trail and fell running around the Lake District, as well as providing a brief grounding in the safety aspects, training and equipment to consider. The key focus has been to keep this book as portable and condensed as possible, to ensure that it always earns a space in your running bag. It's outside the scope of this book to provide a comprehensive manual about mountain running, but the information given in the introduction, as well as the individual tips included within the routes, will give you some great ideas to try out, while the focus is on showing you the best places to run.

THE LAKE DISTRICT

Cumbria is a young county, largely formed in 1974 out of sections of Cumberland, Westmorland and Lancashire. It contains the Lake District National Park, which was created in 1951 and is the largest and most visited national park in England with over 16 million annual visitors. In 2016 the national park's bid for World Heritage Status was submitted to UNESCO, and a decision is due in 2017.

There is a strong Roman and Viking legacy in the Lakes, but the mountains of the Lake District were a poor upland area before a massive growth in tourism brought huge changes and wealth to the region. The Lakes poets – Wordsworth, Coleridge and Southey – lived in the region at the turn of the 19th century and their writings brought notoriety to the area, as well as the first tourists. The Industrial Revolution also saw many cotton mill owners and industrialists building large residences.

Tourism has increased further in the region since the creation of the national park, with its lakes and mountains providing a perfect setting for outdoor activities. Sporting events ranging from the Fred Whitton cycle race to the Great North Swim, Brathay Marathon and Lakes in a Day races are hosted locally each year, confirming the reputation of the area as a mecca for sports. More recently, world-class running events have been

Keswick makes a good base for a running holiday

established, including the Lakeland 50 and 100, and the Lakes Sky Ultra. These are huge dates on the local, national, and even the international sporting calendar.

You'd be forgiven for thinking that the numbers of hillwalkers far outnumber those of mountain runners, and while the legacy of Alfred Wainwright is still strong, the fastest growing cohort of mountain users are runners. Trail and fell running has arrived on a massive scale, and is now crucial to the local economy.

Bases for a trail and fell running holiday

The key towns of Windermere, Coniston, Ambleside and Keswick may be of particular interest to runners, but there's a wide range of accommodation available throughout the Lake District. This varies from some excellent campsites and bunkhouses to B&Bs and boutique hotels, so there's something for every budget and taste.

In terms of public transport, the easiest towns in the South Lakes to travel to are Windermere and Ambleside. The train station in Windermere is the end of the branch line from Oxenholme, which connects with the West Coast Main Line. Both Windermere and Ambleside are linked by the National Express and local bus services, so these two towns are great hubs for runners to base themselves in. For the North Lakes the obvious base is Keswick, with bus connections along the A66 from Penrith and Carlisle.

For campers, there are plenty of options available throughout the Lakes, ranging from basic campsites to glamping options complete with tipi. For more details of suggested campsites see Appendix A.

Swinside Inn at the start of Route 22

Signpost on path to Ard Crags

of August. Key peaks in tourist numbers occur around the school half-terms and summer holidays, as well as at weekends with day-trippers. For those seeking a quieter time, early to mid June and the autumn (apart from the half-term) are far less busy; you'll have more accommodation options and you might also have the trails and fells to yourself.

Travelling to the Lake District

By air

The closest international airports to the Lake District are Manchester and Liverpool for the South Lakes, or Newcastle for the North Lakes. They're well served by direct flights from all over Europe, both on national and budget carriers. To search for flights, try www.skyscanner.net. The easiest transport connections are from Manchester airport, where you can get a coach or taxi, or hire a car and drive to the Lakes, or you can take the train to change at Preston and Oxenholme, arriving in Windermere.

By rail

The only train line into the Lake District is the branch line to Windermere. Oxenholme Lake District station links the West Coast Mainline to the Lakes Line and train travel to the region is highly recommended. It takes an average of 3hr 10min to travel from London Euston to Windermere, and the first train in the morning arrives at 09.30am, so a weekend visit or

For those who prefer a roof over their heads, at the cheaper end of the scale there are youth hostels and affordable rooms available in most of the valleys around the national park (see Appendix A). For those to whom proximity to beer is a factor, all the runs in this guidebook start and end at one of the outstanding pubs of the region, and many of them offer accommodation too. Links to all their websites are at the end of this book in Appendix A. The amazing range of great locally brewed ales, and traditional pubs, are inextricably linked to fell running. Just take a look at the pump clip for Jennings Cumberland ale: you'll see the silhouettes of two fell runners.

For more variety and more luxurious accommodation, visit Cumbria Tourism's accommodation finder website (www.golakes.co.uk) where you can specify your requirements and see a list of current availability that can be booked online.

Booking ahead is always recommended – especially in the peak summer season from mid June to the end even a day trip is possible, even from the south-east. Visit Trainline (www.thetrainline.com) to book tickets.

By bus

There's a regular National Express (www.nationalexpress.com) coach service from London Victoria to the Lake District. For those flying to Manchester airport, there's a regular coach service to the Lake District – although this is a lot slower than the train – as well as a range of private taxi companies.

By car

Driving to the Lake District couldn't be simpler, as the M6 motorway cuts past the eastern fringe of the national park. Junction 36 is ideal for access to the South Lakes via the A590 and A591, and Junction 40 gives access to the A66 for entry into the North Lakes.

Travelling around the Lake District

You are strongly urged to travel by public transport where possible, to help reduce congestion and the impact on the Lake District's unique environment, but if you choose to drive remember that parking in some of the valleys is limited, and ask permission first before using pub or hotel car parks. Also be careful parking on roads or in gateways, as it is essential not to block access, especially for the emergency services including Mountain Rescue.

The public transport links around the national park are relatively infrequent, and so some careful planning is required. The council provides online timetables for the region (www.cumbria.gov.uk/landing_page/roadsandtravel.asp), as does Cumbria Tourism (www.golakes.co.uk/travel). You can even hire a low-carbon electric car locally to travel around the area (www.co-wheels.org.uk). See Appendix A for contact details.

In the information box at the start of every route description, look for the Public transport and Parking entries, which detail the nearest transport and car parking options.

Weather and forecasts

The presence of the mountains has a far greater influence on the weather than many lowland runners may be used to. Despite the relatively lowly height of the fell tops, the region is a maritime climate, and the rapid uplift of humid air to nearly 1km above sea level is often enough to condense the air mass and cause rain. The hamlet of Seathwaite in the Borrowdale valley has the dubious accolade of being the wettest inhabited place in the UK, with an average of 3552mm of rain per year!

Many postcards sold in the local shops make joking reference to the amount of rain that falls in the Lake District, and there are even Cumbrian dialect words for various types of rain, such as 'mizzlin' (drizzle) and 'yal watter' (heavy rain) – in much the same way as Eskimos have tens of words for different snow types. The floods of

Perfect weather for a run on Wetherlam (Route 11)

December 2015 did nothing to break the national perception that it rains, a lot, in Cumbria.

The first thing a runner should do each day is check the weather forecast (www.mwis.org.uk/english-welsh-forecast/LD or www.metoffice.gov.uk/public/weather/mountain-forecasts/lake-district) to identify any highlighted risks such as thunder storms or a low freezing level that could result in ice on some of the fells. As ever, the runner needs to adapt their choice of route, as well as the equipment they plan to carry, to the prevailing weather. In the winter months the fell top assessors report from the summit of Helvellyn (www.lakedistrictweatherline.co.uk) on conditions underfoot and the weather.

As well as rain, we do (more often than you might think) get beautiful weather in the Lake District, and these days make every second of the wait worthwhile. It's easy to get sunburnt and dehydrated on the fells, even on cloudy days, so runners need to study the forecasts carefully to decide what to wear, what to carry, and if they need any extra safety kit.

Maps

Each route description is accompanied by a 1:50,000-scale map blown up to 1:40,000 for ease of use, but runners should always carry a separate sheet map of the area in which they're running. For the Lake District there are two key choices of map: Ordnance Survey (1:50,000 or 1:25,000-scale maps) or Harvey (1:40,000-scale map). For micro navigation specific to small areas, you can also get the excellent Yellow Publications (1:16,000-scale maps, www.yellow-publications.co.uk), which are ideal for runners as they fold up very small to fit into your hand or pack. The relevant sheet maps are listed at the start of each route description, and all the maps you'll need are readily available on the internet from retailers such as Stanfords (www.stanfords.co.uk), the Map Shop (www.themapshop.co.uk) as well as in outdoor stores and other places throughout the Lake District.

Never, ever consider relying solely on the mapping provided on a smartphone, due to the lack of phone signal in the fells, the effect on battery life, and the effects of inclement weather. If you have downloaded offline mapping, ensure that your device battery strength is sufficient. Always take a paper map with you when running; it's not there just in case of an emergency, but will help you explore the fells, learn about the region and learn that navigation is quite simple and not the black art it is often perceived to be.

Safety and mountain rescue

Always carry the safety equipment outlined in the checklist below (see 'Trail and fell running kit'). In the event of an accident you're not guaranteed a phone signal, so a good level of autonomy and experience is required for the more remote mountain runs.

Micro navigation skills will enhance your experience of fell running

Help required
Raise both arms
above head
to form a 'Y'

Help not required
Raise one arm above
head and extend the
other downward, to form
the diagonal of an 'N'

Where you can make a call, the emergency phone number is 999. Ask to speak to the Police, then inform them that you need Mountain Rescue. You can register your phone at www. emergencysms.org.uk; this will enable you to contact the emergency services by text when signal strength is weak in the fells.

If you're out of phone signal and you can't move, use your whistle to blow six times in succession each minute. This is the international signal for rescue. If a rescue is likely to be made by helicopter, secure all loose clothing and try to get into an open area free of obstacles, and turn your back to the prevailing wind. When a helicopter approaches, raise both arms above your head in a Y-shape to indicate you're in need of assistance.

If you're running alone, it's always worth letting people know where you're going and what time you plan to return. Many people use social media or email to enable their friends to raise an alarm if they haven't checked back in by a certain time. Remember that in the UK the Mountain Rescue teams are all staffed by unpaid volunteers, and so you should always turn back if in doubt, if you think the conditions are worsening, and never consider a call-out unless you really need it.

Mountain Rescue teams are frequently using smartphone technology and the SARLOC app to pinpoint callers' exact locations. In some cases this has been used to remotely monitor casualties off the hill in case their condition worsens.

Mountain environment

The fells of the Lake District might seem hardy and able to weather the test of time, but the landscape is exceptionally fragile and prone to damage. Path erosion often leaves huge scars across the mountains, visible from afar, and the upland plants and wildlife exist in a tough and marginal ecozone, where any impact is magnified. In many ways runners are the mountain user group that uses the fells with the lowest impact, carrying the least and wearing the most lightweight footwear. Having said this, fell running often strays from the pitched paths and obvious trails, so we must be careful to try and 'leave nothing but our stud marks' on the summits.

When setting out on a mountain run, pack your bag carefully so that no litter can fall out. Ensure that any trash is stashed in a pocket, to be put in litter bins down in the valley floor. There's nothing more infuriating than seeing used gels or bar wrappers in the fells, as it is obvious which community left them. Having said this, on the whole mountain runners are a most diligent and caring mountain user group, and it's no bad thing to set the best example. Shut gates, do not climb over dry stone walls, and follow the countryside code (www. gov.uk/government/publications/ the-countryside-code).

Much of the footpath repairs are undertaken by the Fix the Fells teams (www.fixthefells.co.uk), and if you want to help protect the landscape you can consider a donation or even helping as a volunteer. You can also get involved with the initiatives of the Friends of the Lake District (www.friendsofthelakedistrict.org. uk). Many mountain runners develop a strong connection with the Lake District and want to give something back to the fells that have provided them such joy.

If you plan to run with a dog you must be aware that the fells are grazing areas for sheep such as the iconic Herdwick, and you must ensure that your dog is under control at all times. Lambing season (between March and May) is especially delicate, and heavily pregnant ewes, or newborn lambs, must not be disturbed. Ideally keep

Passing the intake wall on High Pike (Route 3)

Herdwick sheep on the Lakeland fells

your dog on a lead near any livestock, although if running through a field with cows in it, if they chase you, let go of the dog's lead as cattle are more likely to chase your dog than you, and the dog will likely outrun them anyway.

Bio-security is a topic that many trail and fell runners are uneducated on, and some simple steps can be followed to secure the national park from Non-Native Invasive Species (NNIS). Dirty running shoes can transport NNIS to and around the national park without a runner being aware they are doing it. Before travelling to the national park you should wash down your shoes and running kit at home. A quick wash and brushing of your fell shoes only takes a minute, and you should do the same before returning home. Diseases such as ash die back and foot-and-mouth

are easily spread, as are seeds from NNIS including American skunk cabbage and Himalayan balsam. You can download free identification guides from CFINNS (www.cfinns.scrt.co.uk/species-indentification/identification-guides) in order to learn more about bio-security and to consider how runners can do their bit. On a practical note, washing your fell shoes also lengthens their life, as most upland mud is acidic and rots the stitching and fabrics over time.

Local economy

As with any national park, the majority of visitors stay during a relatively short period of the year, and while you may get the impression local businesses are booming in season, it's important to remember that the local economy is fragile too. The region was hit very

On the ridge of Side Pike, above Langdale (Route 20)

hard by foot-and-mouth in 2001, and then by the major floods of 2009 and winter 2015/2016. Without tourism there would be far fewer pubs, restaurants and shops, which we all enjoy the benefits of, so when visiting the area please try and buy locally to support the local economy and keep the village high streets vibrant.

MOUNTAIN RUNNING IN THE LAKE DISTRICT

What's difference between trail and fell running?

This discussion has been the source of many a friendly argument over the years, but there is a simple classification that this book has sought to make. Trail running is following evident bridleways, footpaths and tracks for the duration of the run, where navigation is largely a case of turning left or right at the appropriate junction. Fell running is choosing a runner's line of least resistance across open mountainside, often away from any path, and letting the terrain dictate the best and fastest route. Navigation plays a part in this classification, but it is more a case of fell running requiring a far higher level of mountaincraft and judgement in selecting a line that suits your mountain running skills set. Many runs are not purely one or the other, but what defines this book as especially relevant to the runner is that many of the fell running routes differ greatly from a walking route. You know when you're skilled at fell running as you'll discover the best lines on the fellsides, where the only footprints you see are those of stud marks from fell running shoes.

Trail and fell running kit

While every runner wants to move quickly and lightly in the mountains, it's essential that you carry enough kit to enable self-sufficiency – especially in case of changing weather and emergencies. Inexperienced runners often query the obligatory equipment lists provided by race organisers, but it's important to note that these events are professionally organised, with medical assistance, shelters, aid stations and rescue plans in place. An autonomous runner should always carry the standard obligatory race kit as an absolute minimum, to cater for

Selection of trail and fell running shoes

the fact that the race provisions and safety net are not in place. Many of the Lake District fell races are organised along Fell Running Association (FRA) guidelines, and so their kit list is obligatory (www.fellrunner.org.uk).

Some of the easier and lower-altitude trail running routes in this book can be undertaken wearing road shoes and your normal running clothing, as well as a small running pack, but as you venture higher into the mountains you'll need more clothing and fell running-specific footwear.

The choice of shoes for fell and trail running is open to endless debate, but what you should look for is an outsole with good grip (for on both rock and mud), perhaps a rock plate in the sole, and increased protection around the toe box. Features such as mud or off-trail performance are key in the Lake District, while they don't matter so much in the Alps, for example, where the trails are fairly established and well drained underfoot. Brands that dominate the UK market are Inov8, La Sportiva, Walsh and Salomon. Rugged mountain terrain is no place for minimalist or barefoot shoes, although an increasing number of runners are using maximalist shoes such as Hoka's for trail running-style routes.

A decent running bag is essential, as there's a fair bit of kit to take each day that needs to be readily accessible while you're on the move. Key features that a runner might look for are a capacity of up to 12L, a bladder or water bottle pouch system, accessible stow pockets for snacks, a whistle for emergencies, and compartments to store waterproofs and other items. When purchasing a bag, try packing it with your running kit and then testing it for fit to ensure that it doesn't move on your back. Many fell runners prefer a small waist pouch or bum bag, into which all FRA race essentials can be stowed.

Poles are increasingly being used by runners in the mountains. While they would get in the way during a short fell running route, for a longer race or trail run they are a very useful piece of running kit. Make sure they are portable (some fold down or retract to fit easily into or onto your bag) and have a grip covering an extended section of the shaft to allow for different hand heights on traverses of steeper terrain. There's a wide range of running poles, from telescopic to z-poles and now rigid grip poles, to choose from. Good brands to consider are Grivel, Black Diamond and A2-16. 'Adapting to the fells' (below) outlines some of the benefits and techniques of running with poles in the mountains.

You're strongly advised to take an altimeter when running in the mountains, as it's a very useful and quick navigational tool and will allow you to focus more on the running than poring over a map and compass. Relatively cheap units are built into robust digital watches, such as the Suunto Vector, and there are also mobile phone apps to consider, such as ViewRanger or Strava. GPS units provide altitude figures, but while they don't need recalibrating like watches, the signal might be too weak to give accurate information, such as when you're close to a cliff and satellite signals are hidden by the topography.

Equipment checklist
The following list includes all the items you might run with in the Lake District fells. Don't assume you have to carry it all: runs in different seasons, altitudes and weathers will have vastly contrasting requirements. Equip yourself according to your chosen route and the likely or possible conditions, but bear in mind that the safety kit should be carried as standard.

Basics
- Trail or fell running shoes
- Socks
- Shorts or tights
- T-shirt/long-sleeved top
- Running gloves
- Buff/cap
- Beanie hat
- Sunglasses
- Suncream
- Water bottle/bladder
- Food

Optional items
- Running poles
- Compression calf guards
- Running gaiters
- Insulation and waterproofs

- Waterproof gloves/mitts
- Thermal layer
- Windproof jacket
- Waterproof jacket and trousers
- First aid
- Zinc-oxide/strapping tape
- Wound dressing
- Blister plasters (Compeed or similar)
- Anti-chafing gel

Safety
- Compass
- GPS
- Altimeter
- Map
- Guidebook
- Whistle
- Survival blanket/bag
- Head torch
- Batteries
- Phone

Personal
- Money
- Bank card
- Toilet roll
- Rubbish bag

Winter/skyrunning
- Instep crampons
- Sling/rope
- Karabiner
- Blizzard bag

Adapting to the fells
No matter how experienced you are as a runner, if you have never run in the Lake District before it will be an amazing experience. However, there

Running with small packs of safety kit

are a few things that runners used to smaller hills may find useful when preparing for and running in the Lake District mountains. You don't have to be superhumanly fit to enjoy trail and fell running; you need to be in good condition for running, but also determined and highly adaptable. Adapt your output to the terrain, altitude and length of your run. Some of the best mountain runners aren't the fittest or the fastest, but those with the most tricks up their sleeves, who save energy wherever possible. Remember that laziness and efficiency are the same thing re-marketed!

Getting the best from your body

Build up your core strength for mountain running, as it is key to keeping you stable and improving your reaction speeds to trip hazards on the mountains. Learn to adapt your running style to use different muscle groups in turn so as to rest others. For example, using your gluteus muscles for ascents will rest your quadriceps for a descent.

When running uphill, try to adjust the amount you raise your feet with each step to avoid wasted energy. Your shoes should skim just above the surface of the rocks in order to reduce impact and over-lifting. Where there's a lot of height gain and your calf muscles are hurting, try running more flat-footed for a while; this moves the stress from the lower leg to the quadriceps and gluteus muscle groups. Once the lactic or cramp has left your lower leg, you can run on your forefoot again.

Look carefully at the profile of the route you plan to run. Try and project where you can recuperate, and where you might need to adjust your technique. Knowing what's coming next enables you to manage your energy output better when running uphill.

Be aware that on longer mountain runs it may be more efficient and safer to walk on some steeper sections than it is to run. While you might never dream of doing this on a half-marathon or a fell race, it's sensible and often necessary on steeper sections of the Lake District fells. Even the winners of some races walk some sections.

Food and water

On longer runs it's important to listen to your body and to supply it with the food types it's craving. It is hard to survive a long mountain run on gels alone, as they may make you nauseous. On longer mountain races the food stations supply a wide range of food, including bananas, cakes, cheese, dried meats, energy bars, chocolate and fruits. On longer runs your body needs complex and simple carbohydrates, as well as fats. A mixture of all of these elements is required.

Running with 1L of water per 1000m of height gain is a reasonable equation. Access to water on your route will depend on its geology and aspect; you can't always rely on

plentiful sources for topping up. Be especially careful in selecting water sources in areas where animals are grazing. In the Lake District there are sheep grazing all over the fells, but there tend to be fewer in the sparse grass near the fell tops or on rocky ground, so getting water from a high source, with tumbling aerated water, from streams with a gravel or stony bed, is the best place for filling your water bottles safely without treatment.

Tackling the terrain

When ascending steeper rocky sections or steep grass on the fells, try not to climb on your tiptoes facing directly into the hillside. There are three key reasons for this: firstly, you're putting a lot of strain on your calf muscles which will tire them for running; secondly, you get more traction by turning your foot across a foothold; and thirdly, by turning sideways you're more stable and able to look around for the next moves to make. When scrambling on steeper ground, always try to keep three points of contact at all times so that a slip doesn't become a fall.

On descent, it's easy to lose your pace by braking too much. Try to let the gradient do the work for you, keeping an eye on the descent rate of your altimeter if you have one. Dropping -25m/min is a fast but sustainable rate. Keep your focus for trip hazards while revelling in the pace of the descent. If you see a trip hazard, push upwards and over it, rather than braking to avoid it. Use your momentum to keep yourself safe. If you feel you're falling, try not to brace for impact but let yourself roll; most fall injuries result from runners sticking their limbs out in an attempt to stop their fall.

Running poles

On ascent the poles improve your posture and breathing, as well as aiding rhythm and efficiency. This will in turn aid your recovery, meaning you're better rested to keep a good pace on the steeper sections. In descent, the poles will aid balance and take some stress off the leg muscles and joints – it's thought you can reduce the impact on your knees by around 30% using poles.

You can practise using poles in descent by planting them together to leap over rocks or obstacles, or by planting singly, well ahead of you, to pivot or brace around a corner. Beware never to use wrist straps without a good fall release system, as in the event of a tumble a radial fracture of the wrist is likely.

Night running

All of the routes in this book can easily be completed within the hours of daylight, but some of the most magical times to run in the mountains are as dawn breaks or the sun sets, and so as well as carrying a head torch for safety, you may actually plan to run all or part of one of these routes in the dark. Be aware that although LED

Fell running over Brim Fell (Route 11)

lights are good, they give a 2D effect, so depth perception is reduced. The net effect is that most runners move slower in darkness, so invest in the best light you can afford, and practise night running to improve your speed.

Mountain skills
To be a safe mountain runner you'll need exactly the same skills set as an autonomous hiker in terms of ability on broken mountain terrain, navigation in poor visibility, selecting the best route for the forecast, and remaining adaptable to your performance and the actual mountain conditions. It's far outside the scope of this book to cover all these elements, but don't assume that trail and fell running are simply types of running that happen to be in the mountains. Good mountain skills and judgement are required at all times.

Don't ever be afraid to adapt your plans. The enjoyment of mountain running doesn't necessarily come from a particular objective such as a pass or summit, but from the running itself. If you aren't feeling up to the objective, or the conditions rapidly change, don't feel pressured to continue; adapt your plans accordingly.

Navigation
This guidebook contains clear maps to help with your route planning, with numbered waypoints corresponding to the route descriptions, but it's important to carry a full map of the area at all times for extra detail, and to run with just that in your hand or tucked into an easily accessible pocket on the front of your running bag. Relevant sheet maps are listed in the information box at the start of each route, and the 'Maps' section (above) provides details of where the maps can be bought. If you use an altimeter to help navigate, you should recalibrate it frequently (many path junctions, cols and summits have spot heights on the map), as a navigational error could have serious consequences. In the unlikely event that you do get lost, return to the last known point and work out where you went wrong, as once you're lost, errors tend to compound themselves.

Running guiding and clubs
If you're unsure of your navigation or mountain running skills, consider being led by a qualified mountain professional, who can teach you mountain running techniques and skills, runners' navigation skills, and give you tips on how to select a runner's line on a mountain. In the Lake District, contact Icicle (www.icicle-mountaineering.ltd.uk/trailrunning.html) for guided trail and fell running coaching. Another alternative is to gain experience running with others in a club, such as Ambleside AC (www.amblesideac.org.uk), with whom you can enjoy group training runs on weekday evenings or at the weekends. For more information see Appendix A.

Using this guide

The routes in this guidebook have been selected to offer a wide variety of running styles, in different regions of the Lake District. For simplicity the national park has been split into four areas, which roughly correspond to the Ordnance Survey 1:25,000 maps; south-east, south-west, north-west and north-east.

At the start of each route description is an information box giving the key facts about the route, including the start and end point, distance covered, ascent and descent involved, level of difficulty, the length of time it's likely to take, highest altitude reached, details of relevant maps, and transport info. Most of these routes can be run throughout the year, but you must always be aware of conditions such as deep snow, ice, heavy rain and storms, which might make the route impracticable. In the winter months, it's not uncommon to see as many skiers as runners in the fells, so route choice must be flexible to allow for the conditions. Some of the open fell running lines, are the preference and interpretation of the author, and your line selection may well vary depending on the conditions.

Distance

In trail and fell running, the total distance is not always the best measure of a route – although it's provided in this book as a means of helping you gauge your performance, or to select a suitable run. Distances are given in metric, to fit with maps and electronic devices from GPS units to watches, as well as in imperial. In fact the distance is less important to a mountain runner than the altitude gain or technical grade of the route.

Ascent/descent

The cumulative total ascent and descent is provided for each route. On several routes an opt-out point to truncate a route is mentioned, so you can elect whether to continue or descend. All altitudes are quoted in metres in order to tally with maps and altimeters.

Grades of route

Also included is the grading of the run, which has been categorised into the following levels, so that you may easily select a route grade that suits your aspirations for the day. The types of route have been further broken down into three types of running, so you can select a suitable run for the day.

Trail running

These runs follow paths that are marked on OS maps, and often include sections of long-distance trails such as the Coast to Coast walk and the Cumbria Way. These trails vary from single-track, where runners have to run in single file, to wider trails or bridleways where you can run alongside each other. On the trails, there is often a good level of signage, so navigation is rarely an issue. The

Fell running over Swinescar Pike, with the Langdale Pikes behind

trails help link together the villages and valleys, and were often historic trade and defence routes.

Fell running

This style of running originated in the Lake District mountains and fells. It is where you often avoid trails and paths to take more direct lines across country, to speed your progress. Fell running requires a good ability on broken mountain terrain, as well as the ability to choose a safe and fast line to ascend or descend a mountain. Due to the lack of time spent on paths, a good level of mountain awareness and solid navigation is required.

Skyrunning

These styles of trail are generally located on higher, steeper terrain, where there are few if any signposts, and the ground underfoot is rougher. You will encounter more exposure and drop-offs, where a greater level of mountain skills and good footwork are essential. Often you will reach a mountain summit on this type of route, and some easy scrambling may be required. Some previous experience of scrambling is essential before considering any of these routes.

Level	Trail running	Fell running	Skyrunning
1	Well-marked wider trails, such as along bridleways, with little steeper ground	n/a	n/a
2	Well established trails, with some small areas of rough ground, well signposted	Off-track between distinct identifiable points, non-technical ground underfoot	n/a
3	Single-track trails, with some steeper ground and rougher underfoot, well signposted	Steeper sections, and rougher underfoot, where care is needed to avoid slipping	Easier scrambling, or small sections using hands too, or easy snow patches
4	Single-trail path, and less marked mountain terrain including scree and boulders	Venturing onto steeper ground, where hands might be used on steep pitches	Exposed with scrambling and mountain skills needed, or steeper snow patches
5	Very indistinct path over broken mountain terrain that is hard to run over	Very steep or slippery slopes where route choice and navigation is essential	Very aerial route, with lots of exposure and significant amount of broken terrain

Timings

The average running time has been given for each route, as this will provide a meaningful gauge for most readers. The intention is that the times will suit the majority, but as you progress through the itineraries in this guidebook you'll quickly decide whether you need to adapt the timings to your own speed. A calculation that works well for shorter runs is 8km/h plus 1hr per 1000m ascended.

GPX files

GPX files for all the routes in this book are available as free downloads from www.cicerone.co.uk/880/GPX, for smartphone or GPS device. Remember to take spare batteries for your GPS unit, especially in cold or wet conditions, and always carry a paper map and compass as a backup.

Abbreviations and waypoints

Within the route descriptions, 'left' and 'right' have been abbreviated to L and R, with LH and RH for 'left-hand' and 'right-hand', and 'straight ahead' to SA. Similarly, the four points of the compass have been abbreviated to N, S, E and W. Numbered waypoints on the map relate to the numbered sections of route description. Furthermore, where a named feature also appears on the map, it is shown in **bold** in the route description to help you keep track of where you are along the way and aid navigation.

SOUTH-EAST LAKES

On Loughrigg Fell, Ambleside (Route 1)

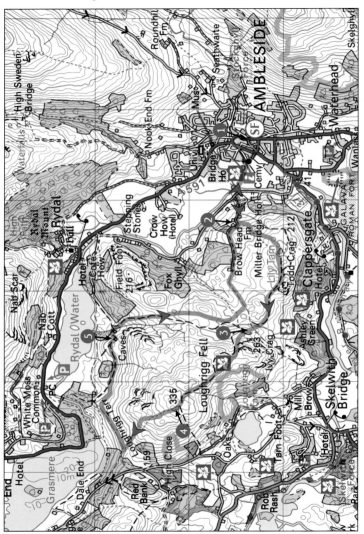

Route 1
Loughrigg Fell circuit

Start/Finish	Royal Oak pub, Ambleside
Distance	9.8km (6 miles)
Ascent/Descent	410m (1345ft)
Grade	Trail running, Level 2
Time	1hr 40min
High point	Loughrigg Fell (335m/1099ft)
Maps	1:25,000 OS Map OL7, 1:40,000 Harvey Lake District
Public transport	Bus 555/599 from Windermere/Keswick
Parking	Pay & display car park on Lake Road

Ambleside is the main tourist hub of the South Lakes, and this short run is a great introduction to the vast range of terrain and running opportunities in the region. While the ascents are relatively modest, you are rewarded with spectacular views such as that of Grasmere from Loughrigg Terrace, and from the summit down the length of Windermere. There are few runs in this book where such great views are rewarded for so little effort, so this is a perfect choice of run for someone who only has a short time available. The name Loughrigg is derived from the Gaelic *lough* meaning lake, and Norse *hyggr* meaning ridge.

1 Turn R out of the pub and run down Church Street to the bottom where the road splits, then run R along the edge of the Crazy Golf course and go SA at the corner into the Churchyard. Exit this in the far R corner, and turn sharp L past the primary school and into Rothay Park. Run straight down the track across the middle of the park, and over Miller Bridge on the far side. Turn R on the road over a cattle grid, then almost immediately L over another grid, to ascend a steep road. Pass the buildings of Loughrigg Brow, and as you pass through the farmyard of **Brow Head Farm** the road turns sharply L, then R.

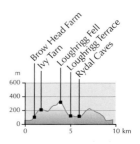

2 At this corner you'll see some stone steps over a wall; take them to reach a footpath that heads off L through the trees. After 100m you'll reach a narrow footbridge to gain access to the open fell. Run up the stepped track SA, and then turn R at the path junction. You'll climb quickly, and you'll soon see a gate through the wall ahead. Beyond this, cross a boggy section before arriving at **Lily Tarn**, with a silver birch tree growing on the island in the middle. Take the track to the R of the tarn, and follow it SA until you reach a wall. Follow this around to the R. Pass through another gate through a wire fence and keep running with the wall on your L until it turns away sharply as you reach a small stream. Cross this and reach the main bridleway track which crosses from Ambleside to Skelwith Bridge.

3 Cross the bridleway and veer slightly R over the marshy ground next to the stream for 200m until you reach a large footpath. Turn L up this path, which climbs directly away from the stream. Follow this obvious trail as it ascends the hillside, gaining 50m of height before the gradient eases and you pass a small valley with three tarns in a row. Just beyond, a wall is visible to your L as you head in a NW direction into a broad, gently rising valley. At its end the path veers slightly L; run up some stone steps to reach the summit of **Loughrigg Fell** (335m). Take in the panoramic views of the Helvellyn range to the N and the Coniston Fells to the W.

4 From the summit, head N and start the descent towards Grasmere. The descent becomes increasingly technical, and on a couple of occasions you may need to use your hands on rocky steps. As you near **Loughrigg Terrace**, run down steep stone steps, then turn R once you reach the main track and follow the balcony track above Grasmere. At the end of the Terrace, keep your eye out for a small track cutting off R. Follow this up and around to

---

Saving the strain

There are some steep sections on this route. When fell running uphill, consciously shorten your stride and aim to use the whole foot in contact with the ground, rather than running on tiptoes, to reduce the strain on your calf muscles. There are two other techniques to try: you can look for stones to support your heel to reduce the angle the foot is hyper-extended by on a steep incline, or on smoother surfaces you can turn your feet slightly outwards across the fall line of the slope.

Grasmere from Loughrigg Terrace

reach a different path, which you follow to reach **Rydal Caves**. These were quarried 200 years ago for local roofing slate and are worth a look.

5 Run down the track below the caves until you cross a stream. Turn R here and ascend a small single-track path, gently heading S. This route climbs over the fell and after 1.5km brings you to the bridleway you crossed earlier. Turn L and go through the gate to follow the rocky path down the hillside. At the next gate you'll pass a house on the L, and at the next gate after that you'll reach a walled track that turns to concrete and tarmac at the corner, where you earlier climbed the steps over the wall. Follow the road all the way down and retrace your initial route back over Miller Bridge and into **Ambleside**.

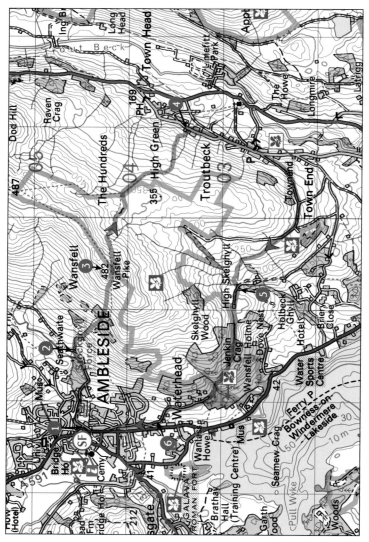

Route 2
Wansfell and Troutbeck

Start/Finish	White Lion pub, Ambleside
Distance	9.8km (6 miles)
Ascent/Descent	475m (1560ft)
Grade	Trail running, Level 2
Time	1hr 45min
High point	Wansfell Pike (482m/1581ft)
Maps	1:25,000 OS Map OL7, 1:40,000 Harvey Lake District
Public transport	Bus 555/599 from Windermere/Keswick
Parking	Pay & display car park on Lake Road

This route follows the ascent of the famous Wansfell Race, which is held annually the day after Boxing Day. The amazing record of 18min 56sec has been held by Kenny Stuart since 1983 for the round trip to the summit: from the start at Bilbo's Café to the finish at the old Kelsick Grammar School. This route is much more than the Wansfell Race, as you explore the SE slopes heading into the Troutbeck valley, with stunning views down Windermere.

1. Turn L out of the pub and folow Stockghyll Lane up past Bilbo's Café, then it curves R and ascends steeply past **Stockghyll Force**. Pass the old school and cross a cattle grid to leave the woodland behind. Follow the farm road for 250m until you see a footpath sign to Wansfell on the right.

2. Cross the stile over the wall and follow the path upwards. Find a sustainable running rhythm, as the ascent is very sustained. As you cross a small footbridge you leave the trees behind and emerge onto the upper fell. As the path crosses a gap in the wall the final section becomes rocky underfoot, and as you near the summit block the path veers around to the L before doubling back on itself to reach the top of **Wansfell Pike**.

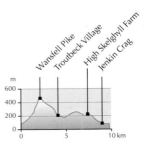

3 Go through the black gate through the fence and continue SA on the path descending to the E. Be careful, as on this section of the descent there are often walkers ascending from Troutbeck. The steep trail soon eases off as you cross some boggy ground and reach the gate to enter the Nanny Lane track. Turn R and follow the walled path down into **Troutbeck village**. The lower section is running on loose gravel, so neat footwork is required, and there is a sharp R then L to enter a farmyard and the road.

4 Turn R along the road and follow it for 800m before turning off R just after the village store and post office, onto Robin Lane. This farm track heads steadily upwards. At the junction with the Hundreds Road, which joins from the R, run SA through the gate and along the trail and across a ford, to reach a farm track at the next gate.

Descending to Troutbeck in the winter

View over Waterhead near Ambleside

5 Turn R and up the hill through the farmyard of **High Skelghyll** Farm, then onwards into **Skelghyll Wood**. The track becomes a little steeper in sections, and it's often wet underfoot. Continue SA past **Jenkin Crag** and around the corner after the bridge over Stencher Beck. The trail emerges from the woods and follows a walled lane, with views down to the L to Waterhead. As you pass the house at Strawberry Bank the track turns to tarmac and descends into **Ambleside**.

6 When you reach Old Lake Road, turn R and run up it until it merges with Lake Road. Continue SA and after 200m you'll see the White Lion pub straight ahead of you.

Route 3
Fairfield Horseshoe

Start/Finish	Golden Rule pub, Ambleside
Distance	19.7km (12¼ miles)
Ascent/Descent	1120m (3675ft)
Grade	Fell running, Level 2
Time	3hr 40min
High point	Fairfield (873m/2864ft)
Maps	1:25,000 OS Map OL7 and OL5, 1:40,000 Harvey Lake District
Public transport	Bus 555/599 from Windermere/Keswick
Parking	Pay & display car park on Lake Road or Rydal Road

This route takes in two major Lakeland summits: Fairfield (873m), and the less frequented fell top of Red Screes (776m). It also takes in seven Wainwrights: Red Screes, Dove Crag, Hart Crag, Fairfield, Great Rigg, Heron Pike and Nab Scar. That only leaves 207 Wainwrights left to run! Another attraction of this route is that it avoids the overly touristy classic trudge up Low Pike and High Pike, which is becoming increasingly eroded, over an environmentally sensitive area of upland bog. The views from the top of Red Screes over Brothers Water to the north are stunning, with the ridgeline of High Hartsop Dodd plunging down into the valley. This route follows sections of the Lakes in a Day and Fairfield Horseshoe fell races.

1 Run up Smithy Brow road, turning R out of the pub, and follow it upwards. The name changes to the Kirkstone Road, and as you head up out of the village, ignore the turns off to the R to Edinboro, the Falls, Seathwaite Lane and

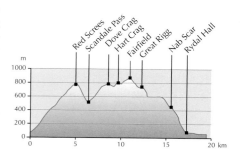

to Roundhill Farm, and continue running up the Kirkstone Road. At the height of 225m, with the summit of **Wansfell** directly across the valley to your R, there is a signpost and a small gate through the wall on the L.

2 As you run through this gate you'll access a wide walled lane leading up onto the fells. Follow this walled track; after 300m it veers in the direction of Snarker Pike, and it ends just above the 500m contour. Follow a wall on the R to the summit of **Snarker Pike**. Don't be tempted to run on the other side of this wall, as there are steep drops down into the stone quarry below.

3 From Snarker Pike the gradient eases off as you veer gently to the R to follow the broad shoulder up to the top of **Red Screes** and its trig point. Turn sharp L and you can look straight down the hillside towards the Scandale Pass. Run down the hillside, keeping just to the wall to your L. The descent is relatively steep, but quite runnable.

4 At the path junction at **Scandale Pass**, continue SA up along the wall until it kinks to the L. Here, cross the wall and the path traverses across to the L up the hillside, passing the tiny Scandale Tarn and heading towards Scandale Head. The terrain underfoot varies from bog to scree, and there is a steep

High Bakestones on Scandale Head

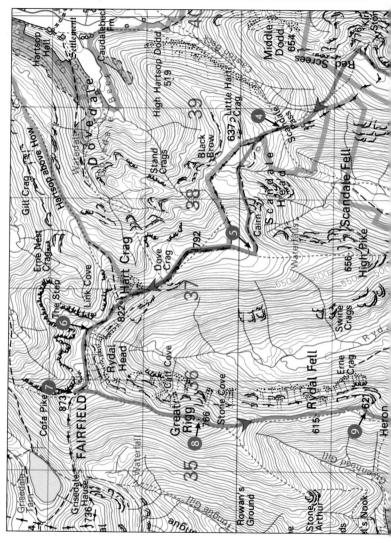

Nearing the top of Hart Crag on Fairfield

stream gully to cross carefully at Bakestones Moss. Ahead, the perfectly formed cairn of **Scandale Head** comes into view. Run past it, and 400m beyond you'll reach the main trod of the unimaginative horseshoe walkers heading N from High Pike to Dove Crag.

5 Turn R and run N to the top of **Dove Crag**. The wall becomes more broken, and is little more than a faint line of stones at this point. The path turns L to a NW direction and there is a wonderful flowing descent to lose 45m of altitude before you start ascending to Hart Crag. This section is rocky, but there's an obvious route through the boulder field. The track skirts around just to the R of the summit of **Hart Crag** – but take it in if you're ticking off the Wainwrights – before a short, steep and technical descent to reach Link Hause. Ahead there is a short rocky step to run through, before the gradient eases and you veer L to run due W. The summit plateau of Fairfield is peppered with small cairns, to help people navigate in poor visibility, so even running this section in fog, snow or the dark is easy.

6 After 600m of running W, the **Fairfield** summit cairn and stone shelter is visible 150m away to the R. Take in the summit views, especially to the

Running Fairfield in winter conditions

Helvellyn group to the N. Some of the best views are actually seen from 200m N of the summit, where the ground starts to drop away steeply, and you can see down to Grisedale Tarn and across to St Sunday Crag.

7 From the summit of Fairfield, run due S across the stony plateau to pick up the main Fairfield Horseshoe track, leading towards Great Rigg. For the first time you'll be running with views of Lake Windermere straight ahead of you. The initial descent is very easy running, followed by a 30m ascent to the top of **Great Rigg**.

8 The far side is a steeper descent, and be careful when you reach the 700m contour to ignore the track leading off R down to Grasmere via Stone Arthur. Continue SA, almost due S, towards Heron Pike. This section provides some amazing running terrain, as the ridge undulates gently and the ground is soft underfoot.

9 From **Heron Pike** the descent is always a bit slippery and tricky underfoot, as you head down through Lord Cove. Just before reaching **Nab Scar**, cross a stile over the wall in a boggy section, before the path veers L. Below are great views down to Rydal Water. The path becomes quite narrow and descends some rocky steps, before reaching a steep stone-pitched path. Follow this down and across another stile at its foot to reach a stone-walled lane that leads down to the farm track of Hart Head Farm.

10 Turn R and run down the track, and down the steep concrete direct road through a corner. Just 100m ahead, turn L onto a walled lane. This brings you behind the main buildings of **Rydal Hall**, into a small courtyard with a tea shop. Cross the bridge, and on the far side the track curves R behind more buildings, then you head L on a farm track.

11 Run along this gated road, known locally as the Coffin Route as it was the route on which the dead of Rydal were once transported to Ambleside's cemetery, which has burial rights. This section of the run is quite flat, and you can stretch your legs after the steep technical descent into Rydal. At the far end of the Coffin Route you'll pass the hydro scheme building, then at the gate lodge house turn L onto the **A591**. Be careful crossing the road, as cars drive too quickly on this bend.

12 Follow the footpath on the far side of the road all the way into **Ambleside**. Just after you pass the Rydal Road car park on your R, you'll see a mini-roundabout; cross the road again to turn L here and run SA up the Smithy Brow road to the welcome sight of the Golden Rule pub, the end of your run.

Looking ahead

On longer routes such as this you need to run as efficiently as possible. Try to look a few steps ahead of you and plan a route through the path of least resistance, rather than looking at your feet and reacting to each step at the last second. A training technique that many runners find useful is to place one of your hands horizontally in front of your chin. This blocks out any views of your feet, and forces you to look ahead, remembering obstacles and adapting to avoid them. An added benefit is that your head becomes more raised, and your windpipe opens, making breathing easier.

Route 4
Stony Cove circuit

Start/Finish	Kirkstone Pass Inn, Kirkstone Pass
Distance	10.6km (6½ miles)
Ascent/Descent	540m (1770ft)
Grade	Fell running, Level 3
Time	2hr
High point	Stony Cove Pike (763m/2503ft)
Maps	1:25,000 OS Map OL7, 1:40,000 Harvey Lake District
Public transport	Bus 508 from Windermere/Penrith
Parking	Car park on W of the A592, opposite Kirkstone Pass Inn

This relatively short route provides a runner with a real variety of terrain, from open fell to steep rock steps, a seldom-visited valley, and farm tracks. You are likely to see herds of deer, as well as flocks of Herdwick sheep, who will look in surprise at runners in their habitat. This run will appeal to those who want to quickly get away from it all, as the starting point is so high.

① Turn R out of the pub and follow the road. Almost immediately on the R again after the pub yard, cross a stile over the fence and gain the fellside. Follow the track up diagonally across the field and through the gate in the wall beyond. The path veers R and upwards, following the wall line up the fellside of **St Raven's Edge**. There are a few rocky steps on the ascent, so adjust your pace accordingly, as the path is squeezed between the crag and the wall edge.

② As the gradient eases off, the path turns L past a cairn and over a small summit of 593m, before descending slightly down some easy rock steps and across some marshy ground. Follow the wall line as it turns R. Cross a boggy hollow before the route

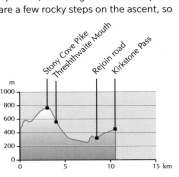

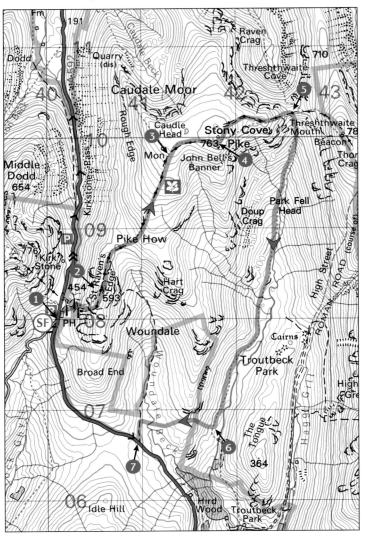

View west from Caudale Moor

gains height steadily on the far side, past **Pike How**, and then the wall veers slightly L. All the time you steadily gain height, until you reach the 740m contour as the wall curves R into an E direction.

3 At this corner, on the L side of the wall, is a cairn with a cross: Mark Atkinson's Monument. There's a plaque set into the cairn, which is inscribed, 'Hic jacet Mark Atkinson of Kirkstone Pass Inn, died 14 June 1930 aged 69 years', and a second plaque reads, 'Also his son William Ion Atkinson, died 2nd April 1987 aged 83 years'. Far below you can see the Kirkstone Pass Inn, which the Atkinson family operated 100 years ago. The view across from here to Red Screes is impressive. Run back to the wall line and follow it to **Stony Cove Pike**.

4 The summit is the high point of your run, but the view here isn't as good as it is elsewhere, as the top of Caudale Moor is wide and rounded. The path continues to the NE from the top, and descends gently at first until it reaches the wall line. Follow this, and the descent becomes progressively steeper; you'll need to use your hands to descend some rock steps. Don't try running it all, as this section isn't a place to take a fall. At the base of the Threshthwaite Crags the path eases until it reaches a pass.

5 Turn sharp R at the path junction at **Threshthwaite Mouth**, and run down into the head of the Troutbeck valley and past the source of the stream that gives it its name. The path is small, and indistinct in places, but it keeps to the R bank of the beck, with the sides of the valley hemmed in by Threshthwaite Crag to the W and Thornthwaite Crag to the E. The descent of this valley is remote, and it's rare to see peo-

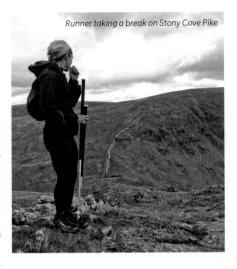

Runner taking a break on Stony Cove Pike

ple. Continue past the waterfalls and cross the wall line at the 300m contour in a marshy section below Black Borrans. Just beyond, pass several sheepfolds and cross another wall, followed by a small ford. Another 200m beyond this, cross a wall, after which you have just over 1km with no stiles or gates as you follow the meandering Troutbeck.

6 When you reach the next wall you'll see the path ahead dropping down to a footbridge. Stop at the wall and turn sharp R up the hillside, and it's a steep 100m climb on faint sheep trods up the wall, crossing to the L side as you work up through the bracken below the crags of High Great Knott. As you reach the wall line heading due S from the steep ground, you'll find a small gate through the wall. Go through this and on the far side run due W across the open fell until you reach the next stone wall. Follow this around to the L and around its corner to the R. Cross the stream, and on the far side of the wall ahead you'll reach a track that heads L to reach the **A592 road**.

7 Turn R and run along the road for 2km to reach the **Kirkstone Pass Inn** again. Be careful running along the road, as it is quite narrow. This final section provides a great warm-down to the run.

Route 5
Kentmere skyline

Start/Finish	Mortal Man pub, Troutbeck
Distance	29.2km (18 miles)
Ascent/Descent	1365m (4480ft)
Grade	Fell running, Level 2
Time	4hr 50min
High point	High Street (828m/2717ft)
Maps	1:25,000 OS Map OL7 and OL5, 1:40,000 Harvey Lake District
Public transport	Bus 508 from Windermere/Penrith
Parking	Car parking along road near pub

This run is quite long, so it's a great training route for those planning to run ultra-trails. It provides many points of historic interest, including the Roman road over High Street, the old Garburn Pass 'road', the birthplace of Bernard Gilpin at the 14th-century Kentmere Hall with its pele tower, and the Badger Rock, famed for bouldering. The route also takes in the summits of nine Wainwrights, with the possibility of short detours to take in a couple more. Best of all is running the western skyline of Kentmere, over the iconic tops of Froswick, Ill Bell and Yoke. In mid July each year, Kendal AAC organises the Kentmere Horseshoe fell race, which this route shares sections of.

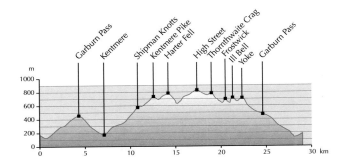

View of the whole Kentmere Horseshoe

1. Turn R out of the pub and start running down the road. Turn R onto Guy Lane, and when you reach a sharp L corner continue SA onto a trail that crosses the fields, heading towards the obvious square stone tower of Troutbeck church. Reach a small road just before the church and follow it L to meet the main **A592 road**.

2. Turn R down the road, and 100m after Church Bridge turn L up a steep walled gravel track. This leads past the buildings at **The Howe**, after which it turns L back on itself. At the intersection after 600m, continue SA on the upper track, and at the 280m contour you'll join the main Garburn track. This was once the main road from Troutbeck to Kentmere, until toll roads were built.

3. Run up the Garburn track as it ascends into the fells. You'll pass some disused quarries before the track curves E, then you'll reach the **Garburn Pass** at 447m. Before you start the descent, spot the tracks joining from the N, which you'll run down in your descent from Yoke later in the day. Ignore these trails for now, and run SA down the Garburn track towards Kentmere. After you round the corner of Crabtree Brow, Kentmere Hall and its tower are visible down to your right.

4. When the Garburn track reaches the road head, continue along it until you round the corner past Kentmere church. Immediately after you cross the bridge, turn L up the road, then take the second footpath on the R to cross the field and the steps over the wall at the far side, next to the farm. At the

small village green in **Kentmere**, turn L and run up the small road, and as you reach the end of the buildings the footpath up onto the fells is on the R.

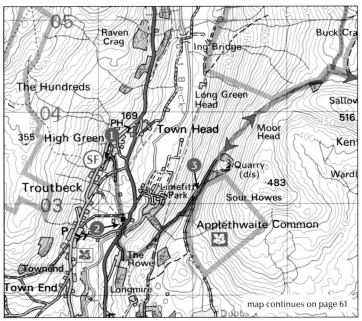

map continues on page 61

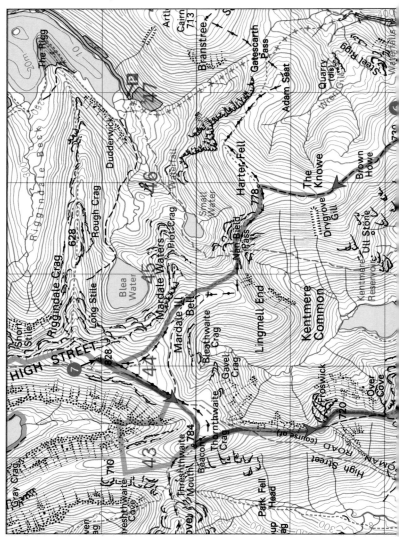

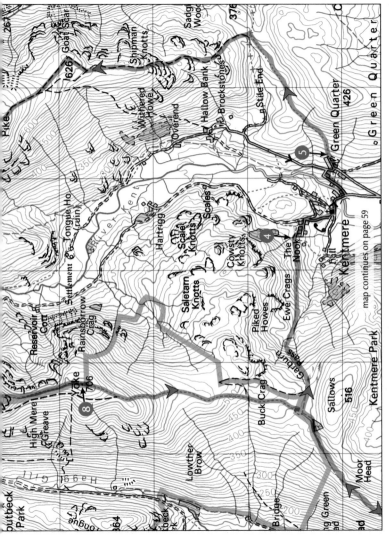

map continues on page 59

5 Follow the path up the fellside and past the sheepfolds at 310m. When you reach the pass at 345m, turn L and head N up the path alongside a small stream. Ascend the broad shoulder of the mountain and soon reach the top of **Shipman Knotts** (587m). On the far side, run down and kink slightly L around the steep valley dropping down to the R. Ascend to the summit cairn above **Goat Scar**, and then run in a NW direction towards the obvious broad bulk of **Kentmere Pike** to reach its summit (730m).

6 On the far side of the summit, lose about 30m of height but keep on running up the shoulder as it turns slowly to the N, until you reach the cairn on **Harter Fell** at 778m. Here turn L and head W down the narrow spur to reach the stone shelter on **Nan Bield Pass**. Continue up the far side of the saddle towards **Mardale Ill Bell** (760m). Blea Water is far below you, down to the R. Continue NW until you meet the main Roman road that veers R to reach the top of **High Street** (828m), and the OS trig point.

7 Turn around and run back down the Roman road until you see the stone tower beacon of **Thornthwaite Crag** (784m) off to your R, and run to reach it. From this summit, a line of old metal fence posts leads S to rejoin the crest of the horseshoe. Keep on the ridgeline and follow it over the summit of **Froswick** (720m) before losing 75m to reach the pass on the far side above **Over Cove**. Run SE up the ridge to the finely shaped top of **Ill Bell** (757m), whose summit is littered with cairns, then down on the far side before the slight rise to **Yoke** (706m). On very windy days the three summits of Froswick, Ill Bell and Yoke can be turned to the R on the west-facing slopes, on the fell runners' paths that contour around the mountain.

8 From Yoke, the path heads roughly S down the broad shoulder of the fellside for 2.5km to the **Garburn Pass** and the track you ran up earlier. Turn R and retrace your route to the end at the Mortal Man pub in **Troutbeck**.

Route 6
Windermere and Kentmere

Start/Finish	The Elleray pub, Windermere
Distance	19.7km (12¼ miles)
Ascent/Descent	540m (1770ft)
Grade	Trail running, Level 1
Time	3hr 5min
High point	Garburn Pass (447m/1467ft)
Maps	1:25,000 OS Map OL7, 1:40,000 Harvey Lake District
Public transport	Multiple bus and train connections
Parking	Pay & display parking in Windermere

This run is great on bad weather days, or even in the winter, as it is largely on good trails and bridleways and so is mostly good underfoot. In addition, it benefits from gradual and modest height gains, so is an ideal choice for those seeking a less physically challenging option. Despite this, the views from Dubbs Lane, the Garburn Pass and Orrest Head have got to rank as some of the best for the least effort in the whole Lake District.

1 Turn L out of the pub, then at the road junction turn R and run up towards the NatWest bank ahead of you on the corner with Church Street. Turn L at the bank and cross the busy A591 on the pedestrian crossing outside the Icicle mountain store. On the far side is a signboard indicating the route to Orrest Head. Run up the lane for 75m and then turn L onto a smaller walled track that leads up into the woods.

2 When you reach the signpost for the Troutbeck road, turn R and head upwards on the stony path between moss-clad walls. Reach the edge of the woods next to a

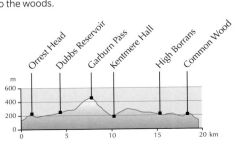

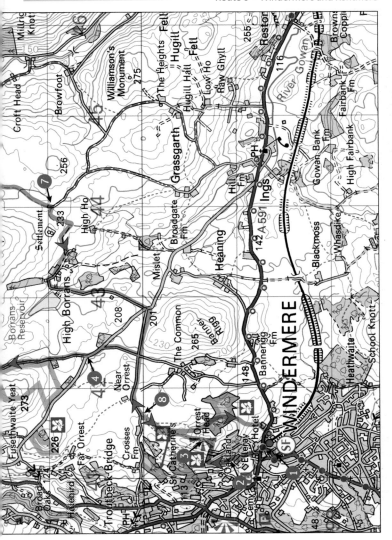

Rainbow over Windermere, Orrest Head

gate and run up wooden steps to reach a kissing gate, where you turn L and run up a small rocky step to reach the top of **Orrest Head** (238m). The viewing table indicates all the names of the peaks laid out before you, from the Coniston and Langdale Fells to the W, to the Helvellyn group to the N, and the Howgills in the E.

3 From the summit, run SA down the far side, and after 150m cross a stile and run across a field on its far side. After 0.5km a path joins yours from the R, and another from the L, before you reach the road 150m to the E of Causeway Farm. Turn R and run along the road for 650m until you reach a crossroads, where you turn L and run 400m to the next junction. Turn L again, and after 200m turn R onto the gravelled track of Dubbs Lane.

4 Follow the lane past **Dubbs Reservoir** and onwards for 1.25km as it curves around to the R above the Troutbeck valley. Just after a coppice, a lower track comes up to join the main track before a gate. Run SA and follow the Garburn track upwards to cross the **Garburn Pass** (447m).

5 Start the descent along the Garburn track, which becomes quite steep as you drop into the valley of Kentmere Hall Gill, before it eases off as you run

down Crabtree Brow. Down to the R you can see the tower of the historic Kentmere Hall. As the track approaches the village, run past the first building then turn immediately R behind it to double back on yourself, following the footpath signposted to Kentmere Hall.

6 At the **Hall**, you'll reach the road head at Hodgson Brow. Turn R and take the trail that curves upwards to the L, climbing the fellside above **Hall Wood**. After 1.2km the path curves around Whiteside End to contour around the bowl of the hillside. At the far side, at the sheepfold at 270m next to a wall, the path splits. Ignore the turn to the L and run SA. Follow the farm track down through several wall junctions, past Mickle Moss to the lane junction 500m beyond.

7 Turn R, and after 100m turn L at the junction. Run a further 300m before turning R towards **High Borrans**. At the buildings you'll reach Borrans Lane, which curves around below the reservoir. Follow the lane until you reach the road, where you turn L, then almost immediately turn R down a smaller road. You'll reach the crossroads you encountered earlier (point 3); run SA and retrace your outward route back towards Orrest Head.

8 As you leave the road and start running across the fields, look out for a path junction after 200m. Here head almost due S, skirting around to the L of **Orrest Head**. Enter Common Wood, then the path emerges into fields on the far side. Run down the fields alongside the wall line and enter a gated track at the bottom, which cuts R and straight down to the main **A591 road**. Turn R and run to the Windermere Hotel, and onwards to reach the pedestrian crossing opposite the Icicle mountain store that you used earlier. Retrace your initial route back to finish at the pub in **Windermere**.

Final adjustments

After a few minutes of running – especially on a hard surface such as the roads at the start of this route – double-check the straps of your running pack, as once the contents have settled you may need to stop the pack moving on your back to avoid chaffing. For most days, the heaviest item in your running pack is likely to be water, and you can inhibit movement by squeezing all the air out of a bladder hydration system, or packing water bottles vertically to reduce the effect of water sloshing from side to side.

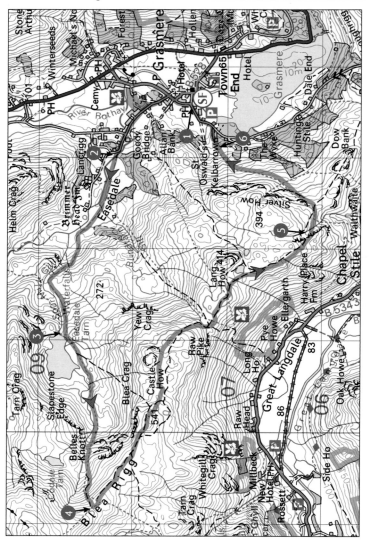

Route 7
Easedale and Blea Rigg

Start/Finish	Tweedies Bar pub, Grasmere
Distance	11.9km (7½ miles)
Ascent/Descent	520m (1705ft)
Grade	Fell running, Level 2
Time	2hr 10min
High point	Pile of Stones (585m/1919ft)
Maps	1:25,000 OS Map OL7 and OL6, 1:40,000 Harvey Lake District
Public transport	Bus 555/599 from Windermere/Keswick
Parking	Pay & display parking in Grasmere

This run provides a bit of everything, from wide trails to mountain tarns, ridges and open fells. Visually it's stunning, and is right in the heart of the Lake District. The route starts and ends in the picturesque village of Grasmere, but don't worry – you'll leave the coach-loads of camera-laden unfit tourists far behind to gawp at Wordsworth's Dove Cottage, and will discover the landscapes that provided the real inspiration to the poets of that era. The only word of warning for this route is that in poor visibility the route-finding over the Silver How region has caught people out over the years, so some runners' navigation skills are required.

1. Turn R out of Tweedies and run along Broadgate, past the Red Lion on the corner and onto the main road alongside the village green. At the far side, opposite Sam Read's shop, is a L turn onto Easedale Road, which you run up for 1km. Run past the turnoff to the Youth Hostel and continue SA to a sharp R corner next to Easedale Beck. On the L is a footbridge, which you cross to gain a stone track that leads up the centre of the Easedale valley.

2. Run on past New Bridge, and then **Brimmer Head Farm**, on the track that's well signposted to Easedale Tarn. Beyond the level of the farm, the path steepens slightly to contour upwards up the fellside, towards the aptly named **Sourmilk Gill Waterfalls**. Run up past them in a steep section of the valley before the path eases as you veer to the L up a gently rising

section of fell, which emerges quite suddenly next to **Easedale Tarn**. Its position is guarded by the austere bulk of Tarn Crag and Slapestone Edge on the far side, and the dank, brooding mass of Eagle and Blea Crags to the S. If you're hot after the run up to the tarn, this is one of the most popular spots for wild swimming, and the crystal-clear waters allow you to see fish below you while you're taking a dip.

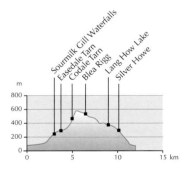

3 After taking in the view, follow the path around the S edge of the tarn and onwards in a W direction. Gain height steeply next to Eagle Crag, where the rocks are often slippery, so take extra care. After this steeper section the path eases slightly, and soon you can see **Codale Tarn** across to your R,

Easedale Tarn, with Eagle and Tarn Crags beyond

tucked behind **Belles Knott**. Ascend further until you reach a path junction at 585m, where the ground drops off ahead of you. You're rewarded with views to Pavey Ark and Harrison Stickle.

4   Turn L and run in a SE direction, directly away from Sergeant Man, towards Blea Rigg. The path braids slightly, but the routes all converge on the SE corner of **Blea Rigg** at the 490m contour. Run E past some small tarns over boggy ground, to Little Castle How and then **Raw Pike**, where the path veers R and descends to the marshy col of Swinescar Hause. Continue SA, heading SE past the knoll of Swinescar Pike – from which you get great views back to the Langdale Pikes – and continue until you see a reed-covered lake of approximately 100m in diameter, nestled at the foot of **Lang How**. Take the R turn to follow the path to the W of the lake. This follows a balcony perched above the Langdale valley.

5   The path starts to drop to the L down a rocky step to cross Megs Gill, before traversing above steep ground on the far side. Watch your footing here, as a slip would be serious, but the exposure is short-lived and you arrive at a

On the descent into Grasmere

large cairn at a path junction on a grassy flat section just below the rocky ground. Turn L and head on the obvious trail heading NE towards the head of Grasmere. After 500m you'll reach a wall line; follow it below the steep ground of **Silver How**.

6 As buildings come into sight below you, the track passes through several walls and becomes a gravelled lane that reaches the Red Bank road. Turn L and follow it for 400m until you arrive at the road junction with Broadgate. The corner is marked with a Dale Lodge Hotel sign; turn L and run along the road to arrive back where you started in **Grasmere**.

Route 8
Grizedale Forest

Start/Finish	Eagle's Head pub, Satterthwaite
Distance	12.7km (8 miles)
Ascent/Descent	340m (1115ft)
Grade	Trail running, Level 1
Time	1hr 55min
High point	Carron Crag (314m/1030ft)
Maps	1:25,000 OS Map OL7, 1:40,000 Harvey Lake District
Public transport	Nearest bus is 505 to Hawkshead, 4½ miles N of start
Parking	Car parking at end of Moor Lane

On one of those days when there's monsoon-like rain and gale force winds, this running route offers a great option as it's largely on gravelled tracks which drain well, and you're protected from the worst of the wind-blasting by the lower elevation and the forest. Grizedale Forest offers trail runners a seemingly endless numbers of paths to run on. It is wonderfully managed by the Forestry Commission, based from the visitor centre in the forest, who maintain the trails and access for walkers, mountain-bikers and runners. This route shares some of the trails used by the Grizedale Trail 26 race.

1 Turn R out of the pub and run along the road out of Satterthwaite, going over the bridge. Soon after, reach a **car park** on the R, next to the woods, with Moor Lane heading off upwards. Run up the walled lane, which veers R and traverses gently upwards above the village. You're following a section of the Silurian Way, and the Forestry Commission have put in marker posts to assist navigation, with green bands on them. As you enter the main forest, keep right at the first four track junctions.

2 At the fourth junction you're at the S edge of **Scale Green**, and immediately after the track junction is a path off to the L, heading

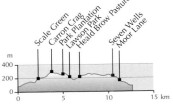

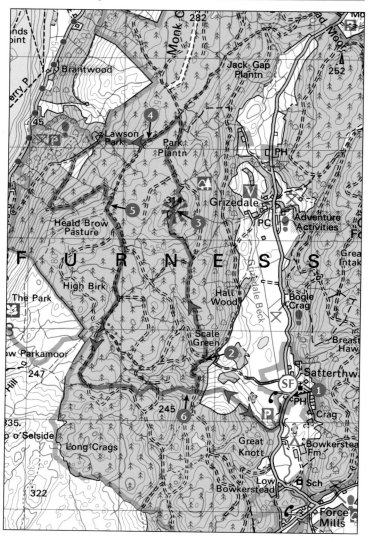

due N up the hillside. Run up this trail, which soon zig-zags up the valley of the Farra Grain stream, to regain the shoulder higher up. As you pass the 200m contour you'll reach a wider track again, and continue N. After 600m a major track joins from the L, before descending a steep track down to the R. Continue SA, and less than 100m after this junction is a signposted track off to the L towards Carron Crag. Follow this until you reach the **summit** at 314m, and take in the panoramic views across to the Coniston Fells to the W and the Howgills to the E.

3 Run onwards and descend the path until you reach a large forestry track on a corner. Turn L and run SA at the junction after 150m, where a track leads off to the L. This section of the route is a great running area, as the surface is good underfoot, and so you can speed up and lengthen your stride. After 750m a track joins in from **Park Plantation** on the R, and 100m after that, turn L at the major track junction and run along the wide bridleway path.

4 As the track starts to descend gently, look for a signposted turn-off to the R, towards Lawson Park. The trail steepens a little as it descends through a delightful section of the woods; keep running down until you emerge at the farm buildings of **Lawson Park**, where you get great views across Coniston Water to the village and fells beyond. Run down the farm track until you see a turn-off to the L, with a barrier blocking vehicle access which you skirt around and run upwards along the path. Follow it around a sharp L bend to double back on yourself, before a rising traverse below **Heald Brow Pasture** and two kinks bring you back onto the main forest track.

5 Turn R along the gravelled track for 1.5km, ignoring one turn-off to the R and two to the L. At the offset crossroads, turn L and immediately R, to effectively continue SA. After a further 600m you'll see a track joining from the

---

Travel light

Much of this route is sheltered by forest and you may need to adjust your layering accordingly. Set off wearing one less layer than you think you'll need; this will avoid you having to stop after five minutes in order to shed a layer and stash it in your running pack. On cooler days, a technical base layer worn next to the skin is essential to help wick moisture away from the skin, while on hotter days some runners prefer a less technical fabric layer (even cotton) that retains moisture to keep them cool.

Gravelled trails are perfect for wet days

R; opposite this, take the small path on the L to the region known as Seven Wells. Cross four steams that feed down into Farra Grain Gill before crossing a forestry track and plunging steeply downwards on the N slopes of Smooth Knott.

6 The path emerges on a forestry track at the 150m contour; turn L then almost immediately R onto Moor Lane, which you ran up earlier. Run down the lane until you reach the road, and turn L to finish the run into **Satterthwaite** village.

Route 9
Black Crag and Tarn Hows

Start/Finish	Drunken Duck pub, Barngates
Distance	8.5km (5¼ miles)
Ascent/Descent	265m (870ft)
Grade	Trail running, Level 2
Time	1hr 20min
High point	Black Crag (322m/1056ft)
Maps	1:25,000 OS Map OL7, 1:40,000 Harvey Lake District
Public transport	Nearest bus is 505 to Skelwith Fold, 1½ miles N of start
Parking	Car parking along road near pub

Black Crag is an interesting peak in that it offers a brilliant viewpoint, and is unconnected by topography to any of the surrounding fells. Despite its modest size, the peak – variously known as Black Crag or Black Fell – found its way into Alfred Wainwright's *Pictorial Guide to the Lakeland Fells*, and merited its own chapter. Tarn Hows is a famed beauty spot for less adventurous tourists, and so this run is best enjoyed at dawn or dusk, or in the winter months. Skating is sometimes possible on the frozen tarns in the winter months. This run can therefore be contemplated by runners in all weathers. The only word of warning is that there are often cattle grazing the fields near Torver Intake, so if running with a dog, be wary.

The start point of the run is the Drunken Duck pub at Barngates. It got its quirky name from Victorian times, when a landlady found several of her ducks on the road and presumed them the dead, when in fact they'd got drunk from a leaking barrel of beer. She only noticed this once they were plucked and nearly in the oven, then knitted them jumpers to keep them warm until their plumage grew again. It's a cautionary tale for runners to plan a pint after, not before the run!

1 Turn L out of the pub and run down the road for 700m until you reach a sharp R corner. On the L is a gateway and a stony track leading up into the woodland. Run up this bridleway, and after 500m you'll see a small path heading off upwards on the R.

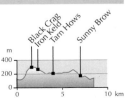

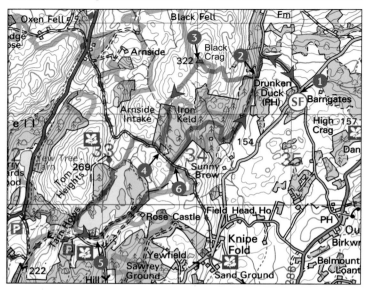

2 Follow this track, which ascends through the trees, gaining 80m quite steeply before it eases off. The trail curves around to the R to contour below some steeper ground, before veering around to the L and up another short steep section. As you reach the top of this, the summit of **Black Crag** is evident ahead of you.

3 From the top, take in the views all around, including ahead to the Langdale Pikes and behind down the length of Windermere. There are various sheep tracks heading in all directions from the summit, but if you head in a SW direction you'll hit a path after 600m; turn L along it until you reach the bridleway to the W of **Iron Keld**. Turn L along this lane and at the path junction after 300m, take the R track to keep on the bridleway trough the Iron Keld Plantation, until you reach a walled lane.

4 Turn sharp R and run along the walled lane, going around a couple of corners, until you see a footpath off to the L. Take this and it soon brings you out to the northerly edge of **Tarn Hows**. Turn R and run along the edge of the

Summit trig point on Black Crag

lake until you reach its southerly tip. On this section you're following part of the Cumbria Way path. Curve around to the L on the trail that contours above the lake edge.

5 Going past the islands, run straight ahead at the path junction until you reach a gate through the wall. Go through it and onto the path that curves around the base of the higher ground of Torver Intake. When you reach the gated lane on the far side, turn L then almost immediately R onto a gravelled track.

6 Follow this track, ignoring a path off to the L, until you cross another wall line as you start to descend. On the far side, keep L on the main track and follow it down until it joins up with a large, flatter track at the bottom of the hill near **Sunny Brow**. Keep L and run N for nearly a kilometre until you reach the road you ran down initially. Turn R and run up it until you reach the pub at **Barngates**.

Easy access

Ensure that you have an easily accessible pocket on your running pack, race vest or waist pouch, so you can get snacks on easy sections and stash rubbish while you're on the move. It's worth practising on a training run, carrying all the mountain safety essentials, before heading into the hills, so you can find out how accessible pockets are when the bag is fully loaded.

Route 10
Claife Heights

Start/Finish	Cuckoo Brow Inn, Far Sawrey
Distance	15.3km (9½ miles)
Ascent/Descent	365m (1200ft)
Grade	Trail running, Level 1
Time	2hr 10min
High point	Latterbarrow Fell (244m/801ft)
Maps	1:25,000 OS Map OL7, 1:40,000 Harvey Lake District
Public transport	Ferry from Windermere to Claife
Parking	Car parking along road near pub

This route is a great choice for a training run, where you want to keep relatively low yet take in a variety of terrain underfoot. The local history of the region is fascinating. Claife Heights is famed as Beatrix Potter country, and you'll also visit Wray Castle, which was built in 1840 and is managed by the National Trust. You'll run past Belle Isle, which was first inhabited by the Roman governor of Galava fort (Ambleside) and more recently by the Curwen family who are related to Fletcher Christian – famed for leading the mutiny on the Bounty against Captain William Bligh. The obelisk on top of Latterbarrow is purportedly a memorial to Beatrix Potter, while the summit itself was described by Wainwright in his book *The Outlying Fells of Lakeland* as 'needing little effort yet yielding much delight'. The views north to Fairfield are stunning at sunset, so this run is perfect for those with a couple of hours available for a shorter run or an evening training session. This route shares some of the tracks used by the Grizedale Trail 26 race.

1 Turn R out of the pub and run along the road for 100m until the road curves L. Here turn R up onto a narrow walled lane past a house driveway. Continue running up this lane SA,

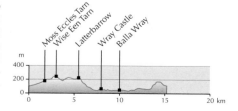

ignoring first a turn-off to the R and then to the L. The track you are on is joined by one from the L; after a further 300m keep R and you soon pass the **Moss Eccles Tarn**.

2 Keep running along the bridleway, where it's usually a bit muddy in places. Ignore two turns off to the R and continue past **Wise Een Tarn** and then Highs Moss Tarn on your R. After 350m, reach a crossroads in the bridleways and turn L. Follow this track past the slight dip across Belle Grange Beck valley and up the far side to reach a path junction with three choices.

3 Turn L and run in a W direction up into the woods. Emerge into a recently cleared section of forest and turn R down a track close to the edge, then go up and over the wall on the incline ahead. On the far side the path turns R, then contours L around the hill past Old Intake. A path joins from the R, and once across a footbridge the path veers L to reach a stile in the corner of the field. Cross this, then turn R and go uphill to reach the top of **Latterbarrow**.

4 From the fell top head off down in a NE direction. The path descends steeply over open fell and then across the wall into the forest again, bringing you to a junction near the National Trust Basecamp, where you turn L and follow the main track until you reach the road at **High Wray**.

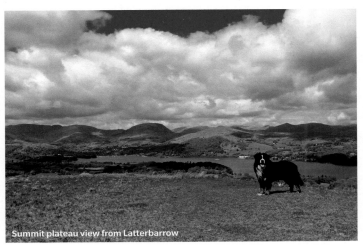
Summit plateau view from Latterbarrow

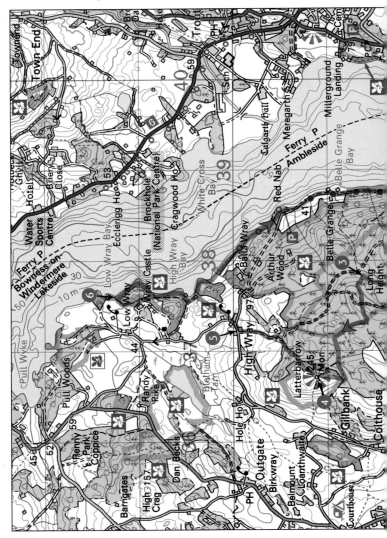

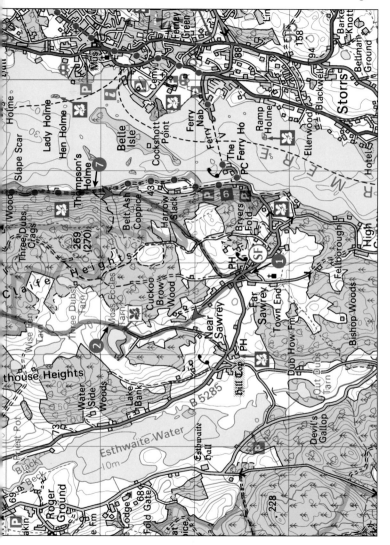

5 Turn R and run along the road past the turn-off signposted to Windermere Ferry, and continue SA past the village hall. Ahead the road curves L and there's a footpath sign at the corner; turn sharp R then L and follow the trail down to reach the lake at **High Wray Bay** next to a boathouse. Turn L and follow the lakeshore trail around and then upwards to reach **Wray Castle**. Run past the Neo-Gothic castle, and at the far end of the car park turn R down a path to reach the lake shore again at **Low Wray Bay**.

6 Turn R and follow the lakeshore trail to the boathouse you saw earlier, and onwards past the **Balla Wray** boathouse, Pinstones Point, **Red Nab**, **Belle Grange Bay**, **Slape Scar** and the Bass How boathouses. This 5km section of the run is virtually flat, and you can take in the views across the lake as the track is wide and good underfoot. As you draw level with **Belle Isle**, the path emerges from the woods into an open field next to the lake.

7 Don't run into the field, but turn uphill to the R and climb up the path ascending away from the lake. You'll gain 100m of height quickly, so a change of cadence is required to switch into your hill gears. As the gradient eases off, ignore a turn-off to the L and run SA across terrain that soon gradually descends ahead of you. As you near **Far Sawrey** the path steepens and turns L into a lane that brings you out onto the road. Turn R and the pub is ahead of you.

SOUTH-WEST LAKES

Negotiating a rock step on Prison Band leading up to Swirl How (Route 13)

Route 11
Old Man of Coniston

Start/Finish	Black Bull pub, Coniston
Distance	14.1km (8¾ miles)
Ascent/Descent	945m (3100ft)
Grade	Fell running, Level 2
Time	2hr 55min
High point	Old Man of Coniston (803m/2635ft)
Maps	1:25,000 OS Map OL6, 1:40,000 Harvey Lake District
Public transport	Bus 505 from Windermere/Ambleside
Parking	Car parking along road near pub

This is one of the most rewarding running routes tackled in this book, as it makes an anti-clockwise circuit of the Coniston Fells, taking in five Wainwrights. There's a huge variety of terrain encountered, from spongy open fellside to rocky scrambling, technical single-track and stepped rocky paths. One of the delights of the Coniston Fells is that despite bearing all the scars of their mining history, they retain a grandeur and solidity that many fells lack. The colours of the slopes in autumn are especially beautiful, with the russet of the bracken, the sharp green of ferns and grass, and the oranges and reds of the copper ore spoil heaps. Across the mountain there are dozens of mine entrances, old buildings, tramways, pumping stations and mining paraphernalia, but it's always the quiet bulk of the Old Man that draws your eyes upwards. The village and mountain get their name from the Norse word *konungr* for king and *tun* for village, thus indicating it was a town that formed a small Viking kingdom in the 12th century. Coniston is the resting place of John Ruskin and Donald Campbell.

1 Turn L out of the pub and run up the road past the Coniston Brewery and Ruskin Museum. The road gives way to a gravelled track that ascends into the Coppermines valley. When the wall on the left stops, there's a steep drop-off to the L into Church Beck, so don't run too close to the edge of the track. Pass the Miners Bridge and continue up the track as it eases off onto a flat valley floor.

2 At the track junction, turn R upwards on the drive towards the row of miners' cottages, and again R upwards before you reach them. This steep track reaches a junction after 150m, where you turn R, then L up the path leading towards Hole Rake. This path follows a long, ascending traverse across the bracken-covered hillside and is well maintained. As the path turns gently

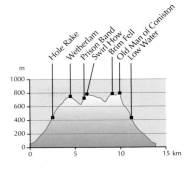

around to the R and starts to ease off in gradient, look out for a small path on the L.

3 This small path drops down from the Hole Rake path, before ascending immediately to work its way up onto the spur of the mountainside to the N. The path is indistinct in places, and braided in others, but as long as you keep on the wide shoulder of the fell, heading N, you are in the right

Running up Wetherlam from Coniston

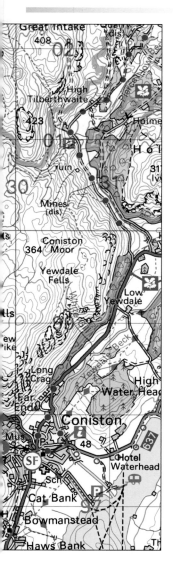

direction. The views L to the Old Man of Coniston are superb on this section, so take them in as you grind on upwards.

4 Most of the routes converge at a little tarn at 630m, where there's a more distinct path to follow up over Lower Lows towards Wetherlam. As you pass the 700m contour, take extra care on a windy day as the trail runs close to some steep drop-offs to the R. After a couple of rocky bands, run across boulders to reach the cairn on the summit of **Wetherlam** (762m).

5 Turn L and run due W, threading your way through the rocks to pick up a track that becomes more distinct as you descend. After passing a steeper rock step, there follows a fast section of running as you traverse above Keld Gill Head. As you run across the steep ground there are some little rocky sections to negotiate, then as you descend to Swirl Hawse it's steeper with loose rock underfoot. Take a quick breather at the cairn: ahead lies the toughest section of the day.

6 Ignore the path heading off to the L and run SA towards the **Prison Band**, up a steep rocky section. Pass to the R side of the ridge initially, and there's a short section where some scrambling may be required. Reach the ridge crest and then remain generally on the L of the ridge to work up a series of easy rocky steps. As you ascend you can look R into the wide gully of Broad Slack, in which you can make out the skeleton of a crashed

The beautiful summit cairn of Swirl How

Handley Page Halifax bomber. Cast your eyes upwards too, as the views to the N of Crinkle Crags and Bowfell come into view.

7 At the summit of **Swirl How** curve around to the R to descend and contour around towards the summit of Great Carrs. On the col you'll pass the landing gear of the Halifax bomber, and a wooden cross memorial to the Canadian flight crew. Take in the summit of **Great Carrs**, another Wainwright fell top, before returning to the memorial and using this as an altitude guideline to follow the contour across the hillside. You'll notice that you aren't the first to do this; there's a faint fell runners' path cutting almost due S across the slope below Swirl How and Swirl Band. Once clear of the crags of Whity Head you can allow yourself to drop into a descending traverse from the 750m contour to 700m, and if you judge it well, you'll arrive at **Levers Hawse**.

8 Run SA along the ridgeline up over **Brim Fell** (796m), and onwards towards the Old Man of Coniston, which comes into view ahead. On a misty or snowy day you can use the series of small cairns along the path to guide you. The summit of the **Old Man** (803m) is marked by a large slate platform and cairn on its top. Anyone that read Arthur Ransome books as a child will recognise this top as Kanchenjunga from the book *Swallowdale*.

9 From the summit, head off to the SE initially, and the path soon turns slightly L to head down the rocky rib. This section has a series of rocky steps to negotiate before a small col is reached, where the path veers L on a rock-pitched path zig-zagging down towards **Low Water**. If your feet and legs are aching by this point, it's a good place for a dip in the cool waters.

10 The path turns R away from the lake and into an interesting section of old mining levels and grading floors, with rusted cable-way wires across the track and ruined buildings. Far from looking like messy industrial relics, there's something inspiring about how previous generations made a hard-fought living from the mountain itself. As you leave the mining relics behind, follow the path downwards but keep an eye out for a track joining from the L at 315m; less than 100m ahead, at the 300m contour, turn off L on a small path.

11 Run along this path through the bracken as it curves R around the hillside and drops gradually towards the beck in the valley floor. Pass through a couple of gates at the wall lines, and eventually arrive at the Miners Bridge, which you passed earlier at the start of the run. Cross the bridge and turn R down the track you ascended. Follow this all the way back into **Coniston**.

Save your shins

This route involves a stretch through bracken: wear calf guards to avoid getting cut – especially in the autumn when the stalks are dry and brittle. When selecting calf guards, there are two schools of thought as to their benefits: firstly as compression wear to facilitate increased circulation and to reduce lactic build-up, and secondly as a less tight fitting layer to keep the calf warmer and to offer protection against bracken, rocks or even crusty snow.

Route 12
Langdale Horseshoe

Start/Finish	Old Dungeon Ghyll pub, Langdale
Distance	19.2km (12 miles)
Ascent/Descent	1310m (4300ft)
Grade	Fell running, Level 4
Time	3hr 50min
High point	Bowfell (902m/2959ft)
Maps	1:25,000 OS Map OL6, 1:40,000 Harvey Lake District
Public transport	Bus 516 from Ambleside/Elterwater
Parking	Pay & display parking next to pub

This is one of the classic Lakeland fell runs, typically raced in early October each year. It's a baptism of fire if you're looking for an introduction to fell running, as it's a half-marathon distance gaining similar height to Ben Nevis. In addition, while it's fairly easy to navigate the circuit, if you're looking for the fastest running 'lines', navigation and route choice are key – and not always straightforward in cloud. However, this is one of the most magnificent fell race routes, and on a fine day there are few better. When taking it at a more leisurely pace you can take in many extra summits too.

1 Turn L immediately out of the pub, and just behind it turn R onto the Cumbria Way path, which leads across towards New Dungeon Ghyll. When the path from the Sticklebarn car park joins from the R, turn L up the hill, following the bank of Stickle Ghyll. The pitched stone path is well maintained and easy to follow; you'll find the quickest route is on the W bank.

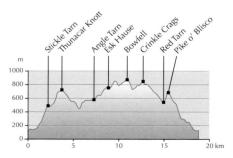

Classic view of the Langdale Pikes

2 As you crest the slope, you arrive at **Stickle Tarn** with a stunning view of Pavey Ark and Jack's Rake ahead. Turn R and cross the beck, and follow the track around the tarn. Bright Beck is in the top R corner of the tarn, coming down to the R of Pavey Ark. Run up the path on the R side of the beck for 200m, then turn L to cross the stream and follow the stony path up the back of Pavey Ark. It's quite rocky underfoot, but still runnable.

3 At the top of **Pavey Ark** the paths braid somewhat, but the summit of **Thunacar Knott** is straight ahead over boggy ground. (It's well worth taking in the tops of Harrison Stickle and Pike of Stickle from here, bearing in mind there's a small scrambling step on the latter.) Run in a W direction – there's a good track to **Martcrag Moor** on the R of the ridge crest.

4 From here the walkers' route bends R via Stake Pass and behind Black and Rosset Crags to Angle Tarn, but the runners' route goes directly W across Langdale Combe – a swarm of drumlins – to pick up a faint path that traverses L beneath **Black Crags** and up through the upper valley of Little Gill before turning L to reach **Angle Tarn**. The views back down the U-shaped Mickleden valley give a strong indication of its glacial past.

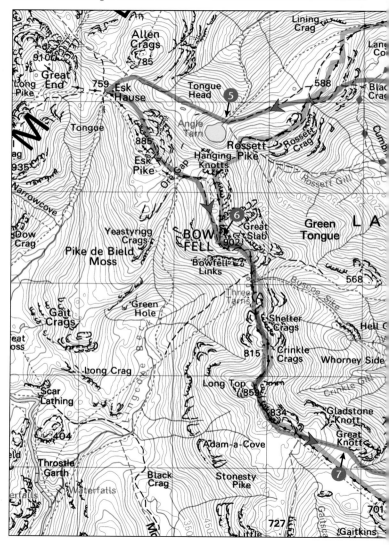

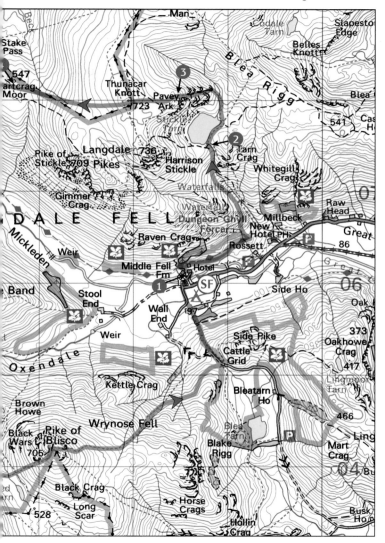

Looking down into the Mickleden valley

5 From Angle Tarn, head up the stepped path to **Esk Hause**. From here there's a route choice to make to reach the summit of Bowfell: most shun the walkers' route over Esk Pike and follow a direct line across the foot of the crags on its NE slopes to reach Ore Gap. Here the summit of **Bowfell** is visible ahead, and the runners' 'line' is straight to it.

6 Head E from the summit of Bowfell and follow the walkers' route down to **Three Tarns**. This section is rocky and can be run quickly, but watch out for startled walkers heading in the opposite direction. From the tarns the route goes S across **Crinkle Crags**. If you keep the ridge crest to your L you'll discover a runners' path that avoids all the rock steps, and which is much faster. It brings you to the most southerly tip of Crinkle Crags, after which you leave the steep ground behind and turn L towards **Great Knott**.

7 Run down the path, or the grass to the side of it, until you pass **Red Tarn**, and then ahead lies the final ascent of the day: up the slopes of **Pike O'Blisco**. From the summit, continue SA along the path down a couple of rock steps. There's a path junction at the 270m contour; take the upper R track, which cuts across the fell in the direction of Side Pike ahead. Follow the path to the road, cross it and take the path on the far side of the wall, heading L and dropping straight down to the NT **campsite**. Here you join the road and follow it to the finish at the Old Dungeon Ghyll.

Route 13
Three Shires loop

Start/Finish	Three Shires Inn, Little Langdale
Distance	18.2km (11¼ miles)
Ascent/Descent	1270m (4170ft)
Grade	Fell running, Level 3
Time	3hr 35min
High point	Swirl How (802m/2638ft)
Maps	1:25,000 OS Map OL6 and OL7, 1:40,000 Harvey Lake District
Public transport	Nearest bus is 516 to Elterwater, 1½ miles N of start
Parking	Limited car parking along road near pub

This run is a great route, as it shuns the key touristy areas of Langdale and Coniston and makes a circuit of the delightful Little Langdale valley. It's called the Three Shires loop because it makes a circuit of the fells that were once part of Lancashire, Westmorland and Cumberland, and passes the stone that marks the point where all three counties once met. This route closely follows that of the Three Shires race, organised by Ambleside AC in mid September each year.

1. Turn R out of the pub and run up the road to the corner, then L down the narrow walled lane. This takes you to the footbridge over the **Brathay**, after which you turn sharp R and follow the lane past Cathedral Quarry and the farm buildings.

2. Just after **Little Langdale Tarn**, turn L at the path junction to keep your height. The path converges with the **Greenburn Beck**. At the wall, turn L and head steeply up the fellside. There's 300m of steep running before a brief respite where a track joins from the L, before continuing up the final steep ascent of Wetherlam Edge to reach the boulder field of the **summit** at 763m.

3. From the summit, veer slightly R and follow the path down over a plateau, then along Keld Gill Head to drop down to Swirl Hause. Ahead lies the **Prison Band** leading up to Swirl How. Keep initially to the R of the ridge crest over

a rock step, then the path traverses to the L side of the ridge. There are a few small rocky steps to negotiate but the ridge is runnable, albeit steep. Suddenly the **Swirl How** summit cairn pops up ahead; run past it and then R around the ridge of Broad Slack to **Great Carrs**. You'll pass the undercarriage of the Halifax bomber that crashed here in WW2, and spot the airframe, which was pushed down into Broad Slack gully.

4 Continue SA along the ridge over **Little Carrs** and Hell Gill Pike, descending over **Wet Side Edge** and onwards down the grassy fellside to the **Three Shire Stone**. This marks the top of the Wrynose Pass road, and the old shire stone is visible next to it.

5 Run SA on the path that leads towards Red Tarn, and after just under 1km from the road you'll pass a sheepfold on your R. Leave the path here and head up the relatively gentle slopes of Pike O'Blisco. (This is far quicker than running to Red Tarn and turning R up the rocky hillside to the summit.) From the twin tops of **Pike O'Blisco**, turn R and run E along the walkers' path, down some rocky steps.

6 At the path junction at the head of Redacre Gill, keep R and head over the fellside around the N lower edge of Blueberry Knott, and curve around R until you can head for the

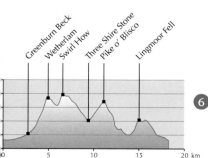

0   5   10   15   20 km

🏃 99

wall that leads along the woodlands to the S edge of **Blea Tarn**. At the gate, turn L then immediately R over the footbridge and continue along the track to the Blea Tarn **car park** next to the road. Turn R and then immediately L up the wall line that leads all the way up to Brown How on **Lingmoor Fell**.

 At Brown How, turn R and run down the broad shoulder past the disused quarries. You can follow the walkers' path that leads down zig-zags past Bield Crag to reach a green lane beyond **Dale End** farm. Run L up the track until you see the footpath sign off R that leads back down to **Wilson Place** farm, and the finish at the pub in **Little Langdale**.

Smoothly does it

This route features one or two steep descents. To reduce the impact on your body in descent, try and run as relaxed as possible. Let your knees bend, to keep your centre of gravity lower, and keep your weight on the forefoot. To reduce the risk of turning an ankle, try to run with your feet slightly turned out, like the hands of a clock at ten to two. This provides a more stable position in event of a slip, but you retain the ability to move in the opposing direction on any step to avoid obstacles.

Fell runners descending Great Carrs

Route 14
Boot and Scafell

Start/Finish	Woolpack Inn, Eskdale
Distance	17.2km (10¾ miles)
Ascent/Descent	910m (2990ft)
Grade	Fell running, Level 2
Time	3hr 5min
High point	Scafell (964m/3163ft)
Maps	1:25,000 OS Map OL6, 1:40,000 Harvey Lake District
Public transport	No nearby public transport links
Parking	Ask in pub to use their car park

This is a great run for those who aren't the strongest of navigators, or who want to avoid rocky ground and enjoy pure fell running on spongy fellsides following well-established paths. It takes in the second highest of all the fells, and on a clear day provides stunning views across to the trilogy of fells that guard Wasdale Head: Yewbarrow, Kirk Fell and Lingmell. While the run may not be very technical, it is a physically challenging route, although there is a shortcut that can be taken in the event of the weather deteriorating on the tops by the time you reach them.

1 From the inn, turn L along the road and then after just over 100m turn L down the lane. Cross the Doctors Bridge and turn R to reach **Low Birker** farm. Turn R here and follow the bridleway alongside the river for just over 1km, passing **Gill Force Waterfall**, until you can turn R towards Boot. Cross the **River Esk** on stepping-stones and pass the pretty St Catherine's Church on the far bank. Continue up the road to the junction at the Brook House Inn.

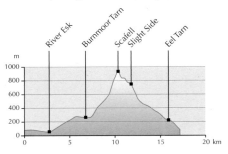

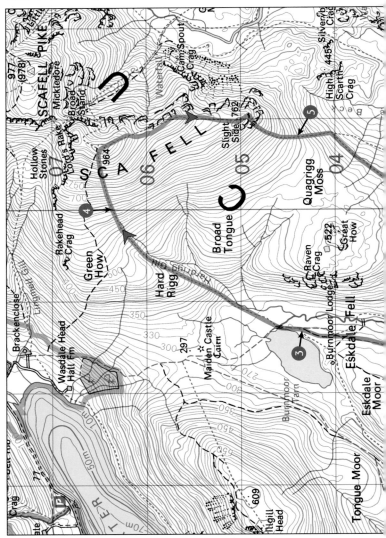

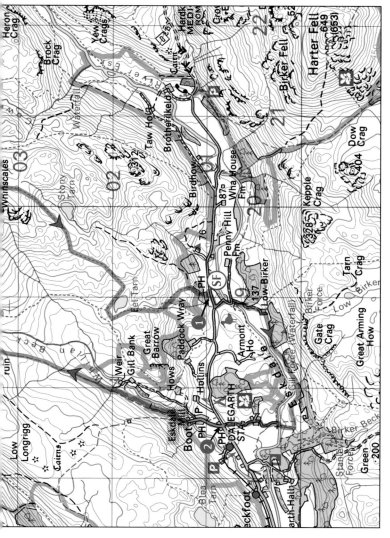

St Catherine's Church in Eskdale

2 Take the road to the R of the inn and run up it into **Boot** village, passing the Boot Inn and continuing upwards past the red phone box and over the bridge on the footpath signposted to Wasdale Head. Leaving the village behind, at the path junction turn R to follow the **Whillan Beck**. This track leads gently upwards through a series of walled fields for just over 1km before emerging onto the open fells of **Eskdale Moor**. Run SA along the path until you reach **Burnamoor Tarn** at 255m.

3 Run past the R edge of the tarn and cross Bulatt Bridge at its far end. Here the Wasdale Head path turns L, but you veer R and upwards, following **Hardrigg Gill** up the spur to the L. At 450m the path turns gently R and crosses several streams as it heads directly towards Scafell. At 650m you pass a sheepfold, and here is the best opt-out if the weather looks inclement ahead. (If this is the case, turn R and contour across the fellside for 1.75km to reach the path descending from Slight Side below Horn Crag.)

4 If the weather is good, continue SA above the sheepfold. The ground becomes stonier underfoot in the last push to the summit of **Scafell**. Here there is a cairn and shelter, which makes an ideal spot for a snack before the

Cruising height

A watch with an altimeter is a great navigational tool – especially on the broad featureless slopes of Scafell. It will lessen the amount of time you need to spend studying a map, as it can give a continuous height reading. Even relatively inexpensive altimeter watches, such as the Suunto Vector, give height accuracy to within 5m and provide details of the rate of ascent or descent, which is a useful gauge of your performance on terrain where the incline has a marked effect on horizontal running speed.

long, steady descent. Turn R and follow the ridge in a generally S direction over Long Green and **Slight Side**.

5 At the 400m contour 1km below Horn Crag, there's a path junction. Take the R fork, which heads SW to the S of the outcrops of **Whinscales**, above Stony Tarn, then down through more outcrops and uneven ground to reach **Eel Tarn**. Keep R to the N edge of the tarn and follow it around to its W edge, then turn L and follow the track leading S down to the 150m contour, where you reach a wall line. Turn L and follow the wall down to reach the **inn** where you started.

Arriving at the mossy Eel Tarn area

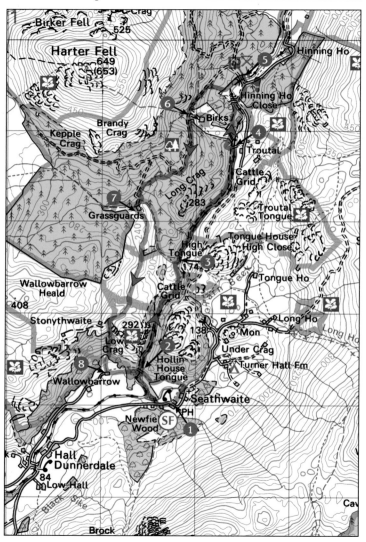

Route 15
Duddon Valley

Start/Finish	Newfield Inn, Seathwaite
Distance	9.8km (6 miles)
Ascent/Descent	230m (755ft)
Grade	Trail running, Level 2
Time	1hr 35min
High point	Dunnerdale Forest (290m/951ft)
Maps	1:25,000 OS Map OL6, 1:40,000 Harvey Lake District
Public transport	No nearby public transport links
Parking	Car parking along road near pub

The upper reaches of the Duddon Valley north of Seathwaite are rarely visited, yet they offer a huge variety of running opportunities. Each year the Duddon Fell race explores the upper rim of the valley over Harter Fell and Swirl How, but this route is more trail running in its character, and it explores the central axis of the valley. It's an ideal choice for a winter run, or if the weather is poor in the higher fells, and several sections are in the shade of woodland so it's also great on a hot summer day.

1 Across the road from the pub is a foot-path between a house and barn. Take this across a field, following signs to the stepping-stones and Memorial Bridge. Run over the footbridge and the path turns L through woodland to cross the River Duddon on the Memorial Bridge. Immediately on the far side turn R to follow the path up the riverbank.

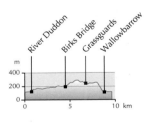

2 The path becomes increasingly rocky underfoot, then it crosses some marshy ground before converging with the river once more. Cross a foot-bridge over a stream that joins from the L, and on your R you'll see a set of stepping-stones across the Duddon. Keep running SA along the riverside path towards Birks Bridge.

Crossing the River Duddon

3 Continue running SA and cross the small stream with the waterfall on your L. You'll run through deciduous beech woodland, then into conifers. At the far end of this you'll see a bridge on your R, which one path crosses. Ignore this and turn L up a smaller path.

4 As you enter a clearing, turn R on the permissive path between the rocks and into the forest again. The path is well marked and it emerges next to a stone road bridge. Cross the river here and follow the road up L for 250m until you turn L over Birks Bridge through a **car park**.

5 On the far side of the bridge a blue sign indicates a bridleway off to the L. Follow this over marshy ground beside the river. Follow the fence until you cross a small stream, then follow the track upwards through a gap in the stone wall. Run SA as you reach a forestry track, ignoring the turn-off to the L. Follow the trail up through the forest, taking the R fork up the hill before the buildings.

6 At the Birks outdoor studies centre, turn L through the gate and up the path, which soon rejoins the forestry track. Turn L and run along the trail, ascending gently through the Dunnerdale Forest. A lot of forestry work and various clearing and planting is undertaken in this region, so take care to note when the path starts to dip and look for a path on the L. Run down this, and it soon joins a wider trail to reach the ford at **Grassguards** farm.

7 Cross the bridge and pass through the gated farmyard to reach a walled lane on the far side. Run along this lane, past ruined buildings and then through a deer gate into a new plantation and more open ground. Follow the trail S and it veers R around the steep ground of Wallbarrow Crag to reach the farm buildings. Follow the blue bridleway arrows L, descending more steeply below the crag alongside Rake Beck.

8 The path plunges into woodland and emerges at **High Wallowbarrow** farm. Follow the signs to Seathwaite, turning L across fields towards the woods ahead. Go through the gate and at the path junction turn R. This brings you out alongside the River Duddon again, and there's a set of stepping-stones to cross the river. Follow the river R downstream and cross a footbridge to emerge from the woods onto a road. Turn L and follow it back to reach the pub at **Seathwaite**.

Mature woodland of lower Dunnerdale

Route 16
Scafell Pike

Start/Finish	Wasdale Head Inn, Wasdale
Distance	34.8km (21½ miles)
Ascent/Descent	2450m (8040ft)
Grade	Fell running, Level 4
Time	6hr 55min
High point	Scafell Pike (978m/3209ft)
Maps	1:25,000 OS Map OL6 and OL4, 1:40,000 Harvey Lake District
Public transport	No nearby public transport links
Parking	Pay & display car park at Wasdale Head

This route closely follows that of the famous Wasdale Fell Race, around the skyline of the Wasdale valley and over the highest peak in England; Scafell Pike (978m). Wasdale boasts the highest mountain and the deepest water. To fell runners, it is also the home of the legend Joss Naylor, who set new standards on the Bob Graham Round with his famous 1975 extended round, which included 72 tops and over 100 miles of running with 38,000ft vertical, in 23hr 20min.

1 Turn R out of the pub and run along the road. At the corner, follow the blue bridleway signs SA over the stile. Be careful not to take the L path following the hordes up the uninspiring three-peaks trudge straight up Scafell Pike. Follow the bridleway across Lingmell Beck, and 500m further on you'll reach the **car park**. Cross over Lingmell Gill and turn L up the track and R to follow the trail signposted to Eskdale. Pass through two fields before emerging above the trees with a wall on your R.

2 Ahead of you is **Illgill Head**; follow either bank of Straighthead Gill up the broad shoulder of the hillside and run up one of the paths to its top. Run SA along the tops, taking care to keep away from the edge as it drops steeply down the crags onto the Wast Water Screes. The contours spread out and you can run fast past the Bell Crag tarns and over **Whin Rigg**. On the far side curve R and cut the corner to rejoin the path that descends the R bank of **Greathall Gill**.

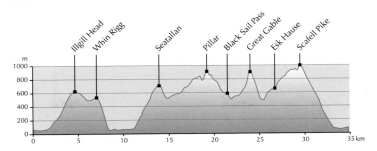

3 When you reach the River Irt, turn L and then R over Lund Bridge. Turn L and cross the road at Woodhow, then run past the tarn before turning R at the next junction, past Ashiness How, and continuing SA to the road crossing at **Greendale**. Here turn R, then after 100m turn L up the footpath towards Greendale Tarn.

4 Run up the hill, and at the 320m contour the stream splits. Take the R fork and cross the stream to its N bank before cutting straight up the fall line of the fell to reach the summit of **Seatallan** (692m). Here you enter a remote section of the route, heading NNW over the marshy ground of the col before veering R below the summit of Haycock to traverse the upper slopes of Nether Beck, passing just N of **Scoat Tarn**.

5 Here you turn **Scoat Fell** to the R, following the path around the top of Black Comb and then veering R to descend to **Wind Gap** before running SA up to **Pillar** (892m). Turn R here and ESE along the ridge down to the **Black Sail Pass**. Here ignore the track R up to Kirk Fell and run SA along the **Boat How** traverse, which ascends around the N aspect of Kirk Fell to rejoin the walkers' route at Beck Head.

Climate control

Arm sleeves are a versatile way of regulating your temperature while running, as they can be raised or lowered without the need to stop and change layers. They're particularly useful for routes such as this, where altitude and temperature change rapidly. In much the same way, Buff-type headwear can be adapted to be worn as a beanie, a balaclava or a headband, to cater for changes in temperature. All of these changes can be made while on the move.

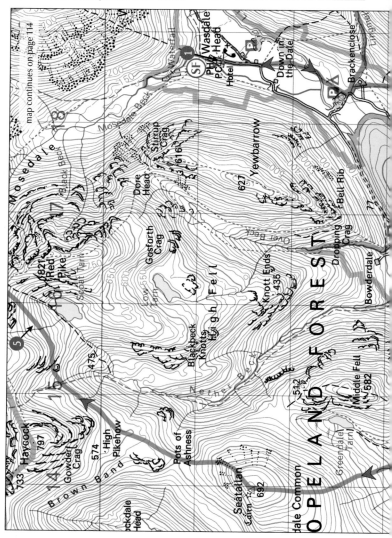

map continues on page 114

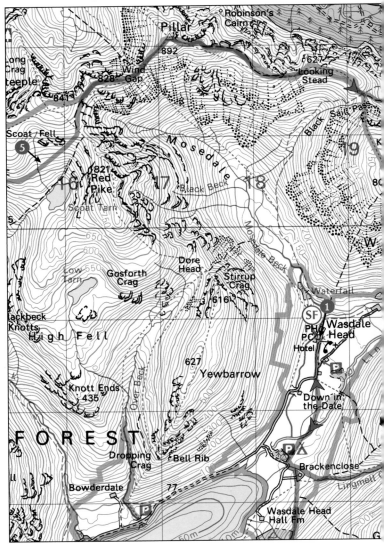

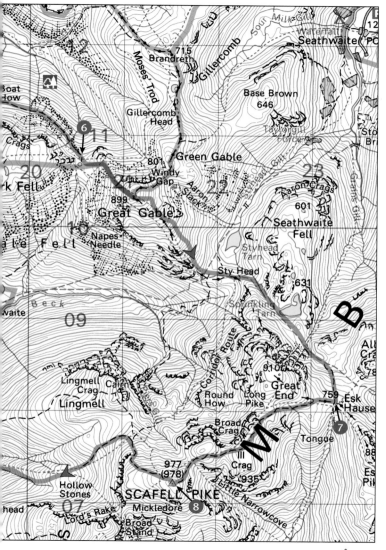

6 The next section involves easier navigation, going up and over **Great Gable** (899m) in a SE traverse to the pass at **Sty Head**. Here, run SA and ignore the Corridor Route turning off R towards Scafell Pike. Run past **Sprinkling Tarn** and up the valley to reach **Esk Hause**.

7 Turn R and follow the increasingly rocky ground up the S slopes of **Great End** to pass over the summit of Broad Crag, before descending to the final col and tackling the final ascent up the NE ridge of **Scafell Pike** to its summit (978m).

8 Having savoured your moment at the highest point in England, turn R and follow the tourist route down over the boulder field. At the 800m contour, ignore the Corridor Route joining from the R and continue SA with Lingmell ahead of you. As the path turns L you'll see Wast Water below. This section of path has been extensively repaired around the **Hollow Stones** region, so be careful to stick to the trail to avoid further erosion. Follow the path all the way down until you arrive at the **car park** you passed earlier, and turn R to follow the bridleway back to the start at **Wasdale Head**.

View of Illgill Head and Wast Water

Route 17
Torver and Walna Scar

Start/Finish	The Sun, Coniston
Distance	10.8km (6¾ miles)
Ascent/Descent	280m (920ft)
Grade	Trail running, Level 1
Time	1hr 45min
High point	Walna Scar Road (298m/978ft)
Maps	1:25,000 OS Map OL6, 1:40,000 Harvey Lake District
Public transport	Bus 505 from Windermere/Ambleside
Parking	Car parking along road near pub

This run is along the lower slopes of the Old Man of Coniston and is a great option for those seeking a lower elevation trail running route, or those with only a couple of hours to spare. It explores the shores of Coniston Water – famed for Donald Campbell's doomed attempt to break the water speed record in his Bluebird boat – as well as passing copper mines. Mining ceased on the mountain in the 1940s, but there are still three active quarries. You will also run along the old Walna Scar road, which connects Seathwaite and Coniston. This route follows some of the race routes of the Lakeland Trails tracks.

1 Run L out of the pub and down the road. When you reach the road junction turn R, then L after the garage into Lake Road. Follow this past the school, and where the road turns L, take the footpath on the R, signposted to Torver and the lake. You're now running on a section of the Cumbria Way, which is very well waymarked. Once across the fields you'll reach the lake near **Coniston Hall**.

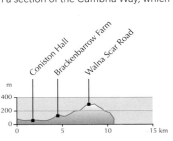

2 Here the path veers inland slightly to pass the campsite, rejoining the shore next to some old ironworks. As soon as you cross a footbridge over a stream, ignore the R turn signposted to

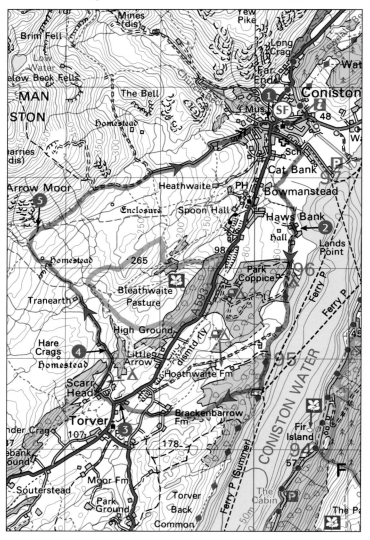

Torver and keep L on the shore edge in the woods. After you pass the jetty, turn R, following the signposted path to Torver. This brings you onto Torver Common and you run past **Brackenbarrow Farm**. Soon after, cross a small road and run SA over the stile and across the field. It's marshy underfoot, and you emerge on the main road through a kissing gate on the far side.

(3) Turn L up the road, and just across the bridge turn R up the small lane sign-posted to the stables and Walna Scar. At the junction, keep L and follow the road past the buildings. The trail turns R and then merges with the bridle-way, which leads upwards towards the Walna Scar Road. Initially the lane is walled on both sides, and you can follow the blue arrows.

(4) Follow the bridleway into increasingly open moorland. Pass a barn, and then a climbing club hut, after which you turn R across the footbridge to the N bank of Torver Beck before turning L to follow it upstream. As the path ascends, pass a waterfall, a disused quarry and a ruined house, continuing onto the fellside. The path braids, but if you keep R it will lead to an intersection with the **Walna Scar Road** at the 300m contour.

(5) Turn R on the wide track and follow it down for 1.5km to reach the high car park, and run SA onto the walled road beyond. Run down this, through a couple of sharp turns, and down a steep wooded descent until suddenly you arrive in **Coniston** village, with the pub straight ahead of you on a corner in the road.

Choose your footwear carefully

There are three principle types of shoe to consider for mountain running; a pure fell shoe, a cross-over shoe that performs on both fell and trail, or a pure trail shoe. When selecting a shoe for this route, bear in mind that the terrain is mixed. It hurts to run long distances on hard tracks in pure fell shoes.

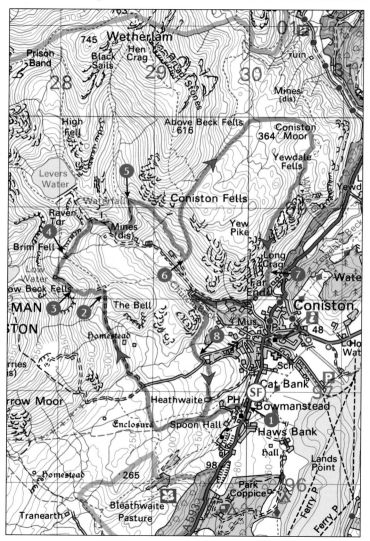

Route 18
Coppermines Valley

Start/Finish	Ship Inn, Bowmanstead
Distance	13.4km (8¼ miles)
Ascent/Descent	630m (2070ft)
Grade	Trail running, Level 3
Time	2hr 25min
High point	Hole Rake (415m/1362ft)
Maps	1:25,000 OS Map OL6, 1:40,000 Harvey Lake District
Public transport	Nearest bus is 505 to Coniston, ½ mile N of start
Parking	Limited car parking in layby on A593

This trail running route explores the Coppermines Valley, and you really get to see some of the industrial heritage of the old mine workings, which provided a hard-fought living for so many local and foreign miners until the 1940s. The running is a nice mixture of wide and single-track trails, and can be enjoyed in all weathers.

1 Turn R out of the pub onto the bridleway that runs in front of its door. Just behind the buildings is where the railway line to Coniston once ran; on the far side of this the bridleway crosses one field before entering a walled lane, which gives way again to an open field. Once you've passed through the gate onto the open fellside, turn R and run along the wall. After 500m you'll reach the **Walna Scar Road** car park, which is incongruous with its wild surrounds. Run SA on the wide track, which makes a gentle rising traverse for 1km, heading N.

2 At a sharp L corner a small track joins from the R, then another track turns off R after 50m. Ignore these two and run SA up the main path. This is where you join the main route up from Coniston, about which Wainwright scathingly wrote in his *Southern Fells*

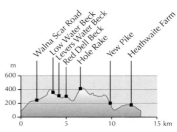

book, 'On this stony parade fancy handbags and painted toenails are as likely to be seen as rucksacks and boots'. Sparing a thought for AW, run uphill past the masses, via three turns in the track to the 390m contour.

3 Ahead the stone-paved track ascends into mine workings. Turn R and contour around the base of the stone spoil heaps, and after 100m reach a ruined stone building that was once the pump house, with its rusted turbine and lathes a testament to the generations of miners who worked there. Turn R and descend the open fellside in front of the building, following a rusted pipe to reach the huge boulder of the Pudding Stone next to **Low Water Beck**.

4 Cross the footbridge and turn R on the far side, heading in a descending and then level traverse along one of the mine drainage channels, dug into the fellside. This path brings you around into the valley of **Levers Water Beck**, which you cross on another footbridge. Turn R on the far side and run past a mine entrance on a larger track, but as it starts to descend, look for another level on the L which contours around Tongue Brow. Run past some old sluice gates that once controlled the water flow on the channel, and on the E side reach Red Dell Beck.

5 Run across the stream and turn R, passing the stone tower and buildings that marked the end of the Bonsor incline and mine workings. Don't be tempted to venture into any of the evident mine workings, as many of the copper veins worked were vertical, and so might contain rotten wooden floors covered by rock debris. These look solid, but are prone to collapse, and often have hollows below them of hundreds of feet. Beware. Run down the track until you pass a row of former miners' cottages below you to the R.

Taking the strain

This route explores a rocky landscape and you should adjust your running accordingly. When ascending on rocky tracks, look for stones to act as heel steppers, to help reduce the strain on your calf muscles. It transitions effort to your upper legs and glutes. From a recovery and efficiency standpoint, lactic acid is slower to build up in the quads and glutes, so engaging these muscle groups is essential for endurance performance. As a top tip for how to trigger your glutes, point the toes of your shoes slightly away from each other. You'll find it's far easier to engage your glutes like this than with your feet parallel to each other.

Trail runners on the Walna Scar Road

6 At the corner just beyond, turn L, and after 50m turn L again, going back on yourself on a rising traverse up the hillside. Follow this as it veers gently R and up to the pass at Hole Rake. Ignore the two paths off to the L and run SA past a small tarn. After a further 750m the main track turns sharply L to descend. Stop here, turn due E and run for 400m. Cross the marshy ground of Yewdale Moss to reach a small path. Continue E for another 350m and you'll meet a path at the 300m contour. Turn R and head S along the path, which descends past Low Wythow and beneath **Yew Pike**.

7 When you reach the wall, turn R along the bridleway until you reach a large track on a corner. Turn R up the track and follow it over a cattle grid to reach Miners Bridge. Turn L over the stone bridge, ignoring the path that turns sharp L and instead running half L up the track. Ascend for 20m on the far side to reach the upper path, heading SE and around the hillside to a corner in the walls. Cross two wall lines to reach a small road.

8 Run SA where the road turns sharp R, and after a further 50m the bridleway turns R to reach **Heathwaite** Farm. Some 200m beyond this you'll reach the bridleway you started out on earlier; turn L and follow it down to **Bowmanstead** to finish.

Route 19
Langstrath loop

Start/Finish	Sticklebarn pub, Langdale
Distance	19.4km (12 miles)
Ascent/Descent	1040m (3410ft)
Grade	Fell running, Level 2
Time	3hr 35min
High point	High Raise (762m/2500ft)
Maps	1:25,000 OS Map OL6 and OL4, 1:40,000 Harvey Lake District
Public transport	Bus 516 from Ambleside
Parking	Pay & display parking across road from pub and National Trust car park

The Langstrath valley is unique in many ways. It is the key valley that links the north and south Lake District, and it does not have a road over it, so it offers a line of weakness that walkers and runners can use without venturing into the higher fells via the Stake Pass. There's evidence of an ancient trade route from the Borrowdale to Langdale valleys via Langsrath and Mickelden. It's arguably also the central hub of the Lake District, seen from a bird's-eye view, from which all the lakes and valleys seem to radiate. To add into the mix, there's a 700-year-old legal battle between the monks of Fountains Abbey and Furness over the Stonethwaite dairy farm in Borrowdale; a hidden cave among the boulders fitted out with sleeping platforms and a chimney; and evidence of Neolithic activity in the vicinity. Langstrath is much more than a hidden valley of the Lake District – it's rich with history, and a great place to run.

1 Turn R out of the pub into the car park, and R again on the path leading behind the pub, up into the field behind. Turn L to reach a gap in the wall, then turn R uphill, ignoring the Cumbria Way track that leads straight ahead. Follow the wall up to the R, then rather than heading up towards Stickle Ghyll, turn L to cross the stream and follow the Mark Gate path above **Raven Crag** towards Loft Crag ahead. Climb quickly to reach the 450m contour, after which there's a flatter plateau before the path steepens and veers R below Loft Crag.

2 As you emerge onto the upper plateau, ignore the turn-off L to Pike of Stickle and head N for 1km to reach the summit of **Thunacar Knott** (723m). Continue SA across a slight saddle and upwards to **High Raise** (762m), then for another 500m to Low White Stones. Here, veer slightly R to descend to the col of **Greenup Edge**.

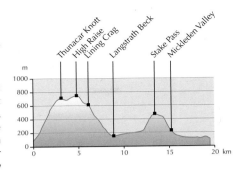

3 Turn L and follow the path down over a steeper descent past **Lining Crag** and down the R bank of **Greenup Gill**. Cross three wall lines, and on your L is a footbridge to cross to the E bank of **Langstrath Beck**. You are now following a section of the Cumbria Way, and it is well maintained underfoot.

Descending past Lining Crag

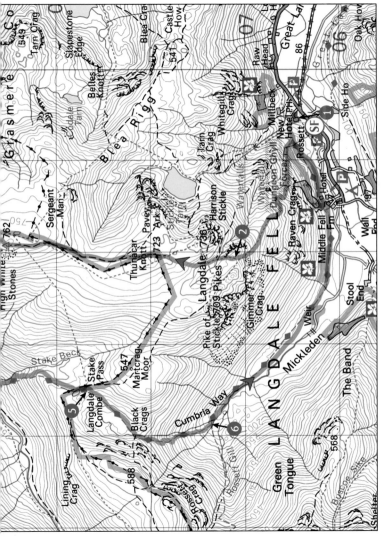

The swimming pools of Black Moss Pot

4 Run up the valley, and if it's a hot day you can stop off at Black Moss Pot, which provides a secluded and great place for a refreshing dip in the beck. Continue up the valley, and at the footbridge over Stake Beck cross onto the W bank to start running up a series of winding bends in the track, which level off near Stake Pass. This area has been the site of some zealous path reconstruction, to help avoid erosion on a sensitive upland bog area.

5 As you cross **Stake Pass** you drop down into **Langdale Combe**, through a glacial landscape of a drumlin swarm. These are former sub-glacial moraine deposition mounds, now grassed over, and they are usually being examined by at least one university fieldwork group. The path steepens to dip alongside Stake Gill, reaching the footbridge at the head of the **Mickelden valley**.

6 Run SE along the main track down the valley for 2km until you reach the first walls. Continue past the sheepfolds and **Middle Fell Farm** to the Old Dungeon Ghyll, and SA along the Cumbria Way track until you reach the New Dungeon Ghyll and the path where you started. Follow this back to the pub.

Route 20
Tilberthwaite loop

Start/Finish	The Britannia pub, Elterwater
Distance	17.2km (10¾ miles)
Ascent/Descent	485m (1590ft)
Grade	Trail running, Level 2
Time	2hr 45min
High point	Side Pike fell (362m/1188ft)
Maps	1:25,000 OS Map OL6 and OL7, 1:40,000 Harvey Lake District
Public transport	Bus 516 from Ambleside
Parking	Car parking along road near pub and National Trust pay & display car park opposite

This loop brings together the Langdale, Little Langdale and Yewdale valleys. It is constantly varied in terms of terrain, ground underfoot and styles of running. There's a mixture of landscapes, from hill farming, open fell, old mine workings, trail and fell. It provides a great training opportunity for all levels of running, with hill sections, technical descents, fast flats and easy trails. It's a route that can be extended, truncated or adapted to suit how you feel.

1 Turn R out of the pub and run across the bridge and past the hostel on the R. After 250m turn R up a walled lane that ascends steeply at first, then levels off gradually. As you reach the top and run along a flatter section, turn off L down the footpath across the fields to **Wilson Place** Farm.

2 At the road turn L, and after 100m turn R through the kissing gate onto the footpath across the field to a footbridge. Follow the lane upwards on the far side through **Stang End** Farm and onwards

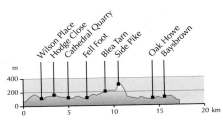

up the track for 1km until you reach the hamlet of **Hodge Close**. As the lane turns sharp R around a house, turn off R down the trail that leads down the field and through a gate at the base.

3 Run down the slate-strewn track and go SA, ignoring a track that joins from the Tilberthwaite slate workings on the L. When you meet another track, turn R and run N along it through **Moss Rigg Wood** until you reach a ford and footbridge. Turn L before the bridge and run along the S bank of the river, past Cathedral Quarry on the L and the pack bridge of Slater Bridge on the R. After the **Low Hall Garth** climbing hut you'll reach a junction in the track; turn R to reach Bridge End.

4 Cross the bridge and follow the lane across the field to a second bridge at the far side, where you join the road at **Fell Foot** Farm. Turn L and run along the road through the farmyard and past the mound of Castle Howe on the R. After 500m further up the road, turn off R along the footpath that contours across Blea Moss below the steeper fellside, curving N to reach a gate through the wall into the woods.

5 Run SA along the path through the woods, enjoying the great views R to **Blea Tarn**. As you leave

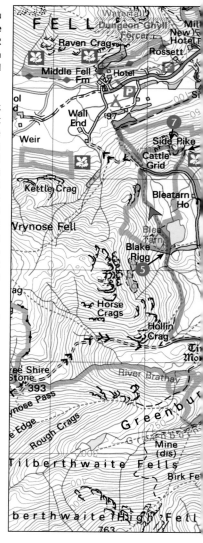

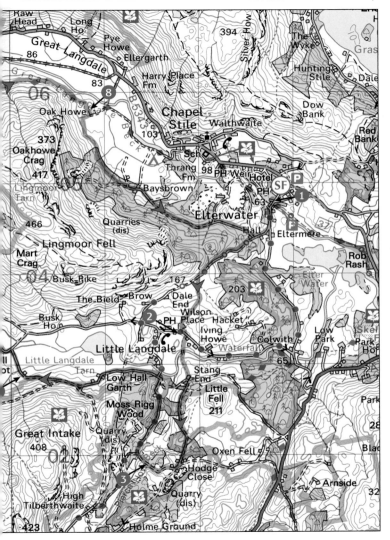

the woods behind, the path climbs gently to reach the road next to a **cattle grid**. Turn R and run along the road for a minute, until you see a signpost on the L indicating the way to Side Pike. Run steeply upwards for 100m, and when you reach the wall, turn L.

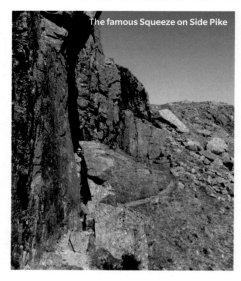
The famous Squeeze on Side Pike

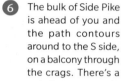 The bulk of Side Pike is ahead of you and the path contours around to the S side, on a balcony through the crags. There's a notorious squeeze between a flake of rock and the crag, which won't prove tricky if you've run some of the routes in this book – unless it's Boxing Day after one too many mince pies. After the squeeze, the path curves around to the R and you can take in the **summit**.

7 From the top, head W along the descent path, following a line of old iron fenceposts down a series of rock steps. As you approach the road, keep this side of the wall and turn R down the fellside. Just before you reach the woods, turn R along the permitted path that contours E to join the Cumbria Way track above **Side House** Farm. Beyond the farm, the path ascends slightly to contour around the N slopes of Lingmoor Fell.

8 At **Oak Howe** turn R and follow the bridleway through **Baysbrown** Farm and onwards into the woods. Keep SA at the path junction with the bridleway heading up the hillside; the track leads onwards to join a track you ran up earlier. Turn L down the trail and then go SA when you reach the road. Cross the bridge, and the pub where you started, in **Elterwater**, is directly ahead of you.

NORTH-WEST LAKES

Classic view of Kirkfell and Wast Water (Route 24)

Route 21
Buttermere and High Stile

Start/Finish	Fish Inn, Buttermere
Distance	21.7km (13½ miles)
Ascent/Descent	1590m (5220ft)
Grade	Fell running, Level 3
Time	4hr 25min
High point	High Stile (806m/2644ft)
Maps	1:25,000 OS Map OL4, 1:40,000 Harvey Lake District
Public transport	No nearby public transport links
Parking	Car parking along road near pub

This fell running route is a great circuit of the beautiful skyline surrounding Buttermere lake, taking in eight Wainwrights and the final few peaks of the Bob Graham Round. It's a big day out, and you're rewarded by a constantly changing landscape, running past the Dubs Hut and Warnscale bothy after passing Innominate Tarn, where Alfred Wainwright's ashes were scattered. There are real contrasts in the region, between remote fell tops, a slate-mining legacy and the history of fell running. This route follows sections of the Darren Holloway Memorial fell race.

1 Turn R out of the pub and start running along the bridleway signposted towards the lake, keeping L at the junction. Cross Buttermere Dubs via the footbridge, and once through the gate on the far side ignore the lakeside trail and head upwards on the path into the coniferous woodland. Cross the stile on the top edge of the woods and emerge onto the fellside, where you follow the pitched path up towards Bleaberry Tarn. This track is unrelenting in its ascent for 250m, until it nears the tarn, where it eases appreciably.

2 The track then turns to the R of the **tarn** and makes a long rising traverse to reach **the saddle** between Dodd and Red Pike, the loose red scree giving a clear indication of where the mountain gained its name. Once the saddle is passed there remains a final 100m of ascent to the summit cairn of **Red Pike**. Stop here for a well-earned break and take in the view of Crummock and Buttermere below.

Low Crag, High Stile and Buttermere

3 Turn S and follow the broad ridge crest along as it turns to the SE over **Chapel Crags**, before ascending again to reach the top of **High Stile** (806m). Rest assured that this is the high point of the run, although it's hard to decide which cairn actually marks the highest point. The path ahead to High Crag is obvious, threading its way along the ridge crest above Comb Crags. Follow it over the top, where it veers slightly R to descend Gamlin End on a pitched track down to the boggy area near **Seat**. Ahead the view is dominated by Haystacks above the notch of Scarth Gap and Warnscale Head. Run ahead down the path to **Scarth Gap** cairn.

4 Make your way SA up towards Haystacks up a track that has quite a lot of loose stone on it, so throttle back and run with care. From the top of

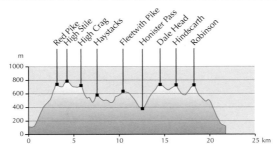

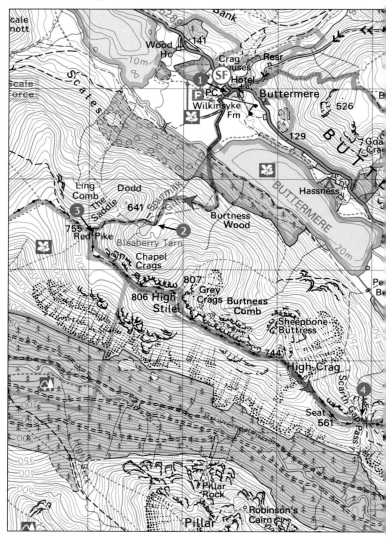

Haystacks the path follows the ridge along to the N shores of Innominate Tarn and **Blackbeck Tarn**, before veering to the NE and along to the stream crossing of Warnscale Beck. On a poor weather day, runners may wish to seek shelter in the Warnscale bothy, to grab a bite to eat or change clothing.

5 As you leave the beck behind you, ignore the tracks heading off down to the L and continue over the open fells towards the summit of Fleetwith Pike. There are many lines a runner can take, but the easiest curves around L above the two obvious streams that run down the hillside. At the **summit**, turn R and follow the track E along the ridge past several small tarns. Be careful you don't get too close to the steep cliffs of Honister Crag on the L, which drop steeply down to the pass. Follow the path down, keeping R to reach the incline from the Drum House down to the **pass**.

6 Here you are following a section of the Bob Graham Round, as you cross the road and stile on the far side and head N up the hillside alongside the fence and onwards to reach **Dale Head**. Turn L and follow the obvious ridge, down the line of the old boundary fenceposts, curving R to take in the summit of **Hindscarth** and then turning back on yourself to contour R around to the top of **Littledale Edge**.

7 Run down to Littledale Head, and SA up the slopes onto the top of **Robinson**. Here look carefully for the path and cairn to the SW, and run down this and onto the softer ground of **Buttermere Moss**. If you've kept your fell shoes dry so far, the chances are that this will end that streak, hence why the route is run in this direction. Continue to the R of High Snockrigg, and at the path junction at the 500m contour turn L and descend quite steeply down to the W. The path zig-zags, and eventually brings you out on the road at **Buttermere**. Follow this down to the church and turn R along the main road, then turn L before the Bridge Hotel to follow the small road back to where you started.

Adjusting to traverses

When traversing across a slope, turn your lower foot slightly downhill for a better stance and greater stability. This technique also reduces the risk of slipping on muddy ground. Climbers will be used to this 'French' technique for wearing crampons, and it has the same benefits for runners: you keep the maximum area of the sole of the shoe in contact with the mountainside, and minimise the risk of slipping.

Route 22
Catbells and High Spy

Start/Finish	Swinside Inn, Newlands valley
Distance	15.8km (9¾ miles)
Ascent/Descent	685m (2250ft)
Grade	Fell running, Level 2
Time	2hr 45min
High point	High Spy (653m/2142ft)
Maps	1:25,000 OS Map OL4, 1:40,000 Harvey Lake District
Public transport	Bus 77A from Keswick to Swinside Green Road
Parking	Ask in pub to use their car park, or drive along the first kilometre of the route to a small car park on the road to Skelgill at NY246211.

This run incorporates a classic traverse over the oft-trod Catbells, before exploring the less-visited Dale Head valley with its abandoned copper and lead mines. This valley is far lesser-known as a mining region than the Coniston Coppermines valley, but its north aspect, overlooked by the Dalehead and Eel crags, gives it a more remote and foreboding feel. This is a run of contrasts, with wonderful ridgelines and views back over Derwent Water and to Skiddaw. It is very runnable with few technical sections. The route is all on paths or trails, so will appeal to those whose navigation isn't the strongest.

1 Turn L out of the pub and follow the main road towards Portinscale for 300m. At the road junction turn R, signposted towards Grange, and follow this for 700m, continuing SA at Swinside Lodge and up the switchbacks to the road junction. Turn R, and immediately on the L you'll see a path heading up the hillside.

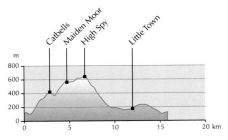

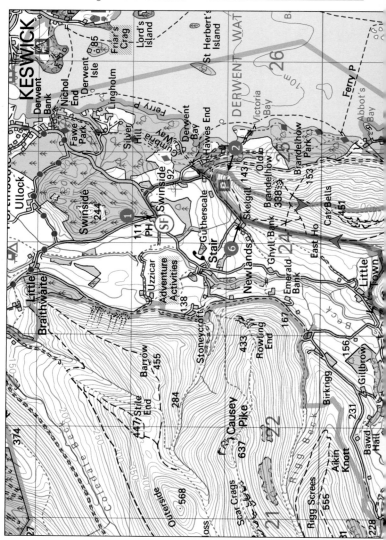

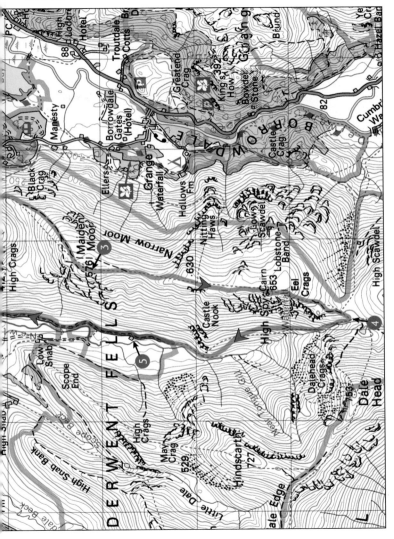

Cat Bells, Maiden Moor and High Spy seen across Derwentwater

2   Run up this and soon emerge onto the ridge leading up towards Skelgill Bank. Follow the crest S over two small dips and onto the top of **Catbells**. Run SA down the grassy slopes to reach Hause Gate, ignoring the paths that drop off to the L and R. Continue onwards up the ridge crest and you'll soon leave the majority of tourists far behind as you ascend over **Maiden Moor**.

3   Follow the ridge S over Narrow Moor and then up a short steeper section, followed by a small dip and the broad ridge up to the top of **High Spy** (653m). The top is marked with a sturdy well-made cylindrical stone cairn. Run ahead down the slopes towards Dalehead Tarn.

4   Before you reach the tarn, turn R down the path keeping to the R banks of Dalehead Beck, and follow it down past the Miners Crag and the waterfalls below Eel Crags. At the 250m contour you'll spot some old copper mine workings on the L bank of the stream; stay on the R bank, where the track veers away from the beck across some marshy ground before converging with the stream 600m later. After turning the corner below **Castle Nook** the path becomes a track and you follow the wall line down the valley past the climbing hut, and SA to the disused Goldscope lead and copper mines.

5   The track continues towards Little Town. Just before you draw level with Chapel Bridge on the road to your L, turn R up the grassy path that curves upwards to the R away from the track you've run down. (Across to your L you'll see the famous Newlands Church, which marks the end of the fell running and the beginning of the final road section for those completing the Bob Graham Round.) Run along the new bridleway as it contours above the buildings before reaching a wall line, which it follows around the N spur

of Looking Crag and into the mining levels and spoil heaps of Yewthwaite. Beyond this the track veers N; run alongside the wall until you reach **Skelgill**.

6 Turn R and run along the road, with the Skiddaw range ahead of you. You'll meet the road on a hairpin that you encountered earlier. Here on the R is the track you ran up at the start of your run: turn L and retrace your steps along the road back to the pub.

Newlands church on the Bob Graham Round

Route 23
Black Sail and Pillar

Start/Finish	Fox and Hounds Inn, Ennerdale Bridge
Distance	33.7km (20 miles)
Ascent/Descent	1205m (3955ft)
Grade	Fell running, Level 3
Time	5hr 25min
High point	Pillar (892m/2927ft)
Maps	1:25,000 OS Map OL4, 1:40,000 Harvey Lake District
Public transport	Bus 31, 32, 217 or 600 from Cleator
Parking	Car parking along road near pub

Ennerdale is set in the quiet western corner of the Lake District and is relatively rarely visited due to the long drive from the motorway – but its remoteness is your reward. The valley floor at the head of the lake saw years of forestry work introducing non-native conifers, but recently a process of re-wilding has started to reintroduce natural species and a landscape that hasn't been seen for hundreds of years. Its southern skyline is a fell runners' paradise, taking in seven Wainwright fell tops, and you follow sections of the Ennerdale Horseshoe fell race.

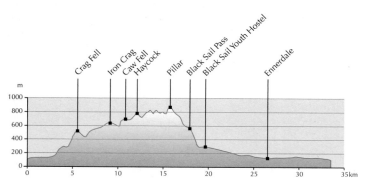

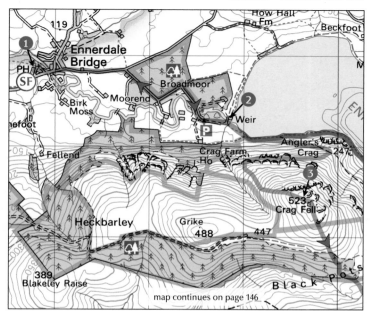

map continues on page 146

1 Turn R out of the pub and cross the small beck, running past the graveyard and play area to the road junction. Turn L and run across the bridge, veering R at the junction to follow the signpost to Ennerdale Water. After 700m turn R at the junction on the edge of **Broadmoor forest** and run along the long straight, followed by a L and R corner. The road crosses a bridge over the River Ehen and curves L to a gate. Go through the kissing gate and follow the track to the outflow from **Ennerdale**.

2 Follow the path along the southern shore of the lake, across a wall line. Soon after you'll spot a path cutting up R towards a small saddle behind **Anglers Crag**. The track turns S and braids up to Revelin Crag. Either path is fine, and they rejoin before joining a track that leads E over **Crag Fell**.

3 The path veers SE and descends towards a conifer plantation. When the path reaches a track, turn L then almost immediately R to emerge from the

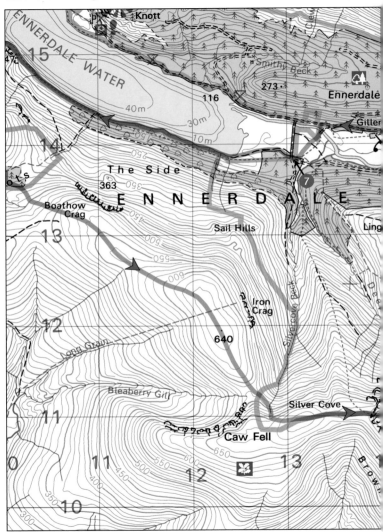

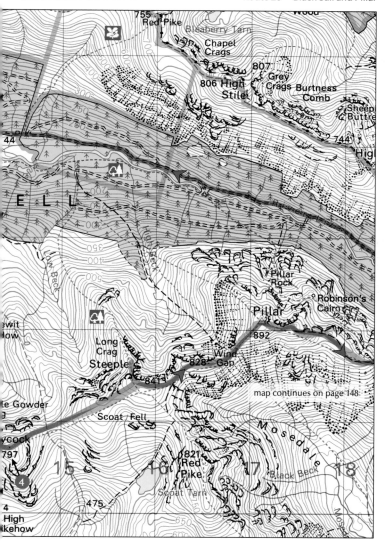

755 Red Pike

Bleaberry Tarn

Chapel Crags

807 Grey Crags

Burtness Comb

806 High Stile

Sheep Buttre

744 Hig

44

E L L

Pillar Rock

Robinson's Cairn

Pillar

892

Long Crag

Wind Gap

828

Steeple

841

map continues on page 148

ewit low

Gowder

Scoat Fell

Mosedale

ycock

797

821 Red Pike

Black Beck

15

16

17

18

4

Scoat Tarn

475

4 High kehow

650

600

forest next to a wall line. Run along this wall up the long slope of **Iron Crag**. Follow the R side of the wall down to Bleaberry Gill Head, and S up to **Caw Fell**. Turn L and run past **Little Gowder Crag** and up to the top of **Haycock**.

4 Run SA down the saddleback ridge and along the wall line to **Scoat Fell**. Here, summit-baggers collecting their Wainwrights might want to divert N to take in **Steeple** (and/or SE to **Red Pike**). From the summit of Scoat Fell the path drops slightly towards Black Crag, and from there through the boulders to the narrow saddle of **Wind Gap**. Continue SA up a steep, almost scrambling section to reach the top of **Pillar** (892m).

5 The ground descends to the E, and several cairns keep you away from the steep drops towards Pillar Rock and the Hind Cove crags on the L. Continue running SA over **Looking Stead**, and past a series of small tarns down to **Black Sail Pass**. Suddenly the ground is softer under your feet – turn L to drop down to the footbridge.

6 Turn L on the far side and run past the spectacularly located **Black Sail Youth Hostel**. The track soon dips into the valley, closely following the

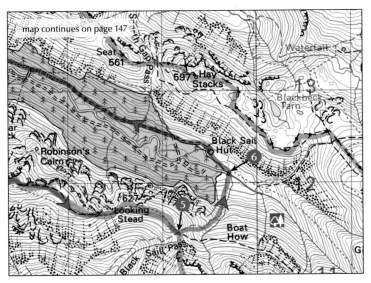

map continues on page 147

Black Sail Youth Hostel

River Liza, and you follow it for several kilometres before reaching the Low Gillerthwaite Field Centre. Just beyond is the bridge over the river on your L, which you cross. All the paths converge from various directions at the foot of Deep Gill Beck.

7. Turn R and go through a succession of gates and woodland to follow the lakeside path along the southern shore of **Ennerdale**, with just one section of scree to negotiate below Robin Hood's Chair headland, before rejoining the path that you initially ran along. Retrace your route along the roads to where you started at **Ennerdale Bridge**.

Get a grip

When the rock is wet and greasy, shorten your stride to reduce the risk of slipping, both when the foot lands at the start of a stride and when pushing off on the next. New shoes are great, but once the rubber of the sole is slightly worn after a few runs you'll find there is better grip than a shiny new pair. Some runners carry poles when it's wet, which gives another point of contact and allows you to use the upper body for some extra propulsion when the feet are slipping and sliding everywhere.

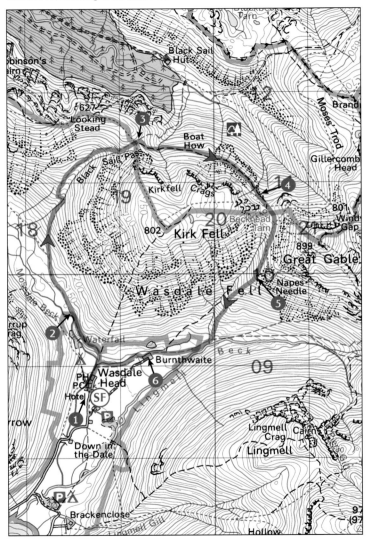

Route 24
Tour of Kirk Fell

Start/Finish	Wasdale Head Inn, Wasdale Head
Distance	8.7km (5½ miles)
Ascent/Descent	580m (1905ft)
Grade	Fell running, Level 2
Time	1hr 50min
High point	Beckhead Tarn (620m/2034ft)
Maps	1:25,000 OS Map OL4 and OL6, 1:40,000 Harvey Lake District
Public transport	No nearby public transport links
Parking	Pay & display car park at Wasdale Head

Kirk Fell stands as a proud guardian at the head of Wasdale, with the tributaries of Mosedale and Lingmell becks meeting at its foot. The huge bulk of its south ridge from Wasdale Head is unrelenting, and unvaried. Worry not, as this run is more trail running in its style, making a tour of this mountain in a girdle traverse around its lower slopes, with relatively low inclines. It's an ideal alternative if the cloud base is low, or the weather inclement. This route is also a great route choice for those with lower navigational abilities, as the tracks are all obvious, even in poor weather.

1 Turn L out of the pub, and after the hotel buildings turn L to reach the edge of the beck. Don't cross the stone packhorse bridge; instead keep on the E bank for 200m to follow the bridleway across Fogmire Beck. The track then crosses above the wall line, where it turns L to follow the **Mosedale Beck** above a series of waterfalls.

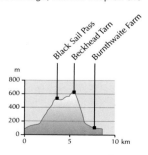

2 As a meander of the beck passes close to the path, gain the open fellside and run along the path for 800m to reach a junction, where you keep R and ascend towards the Gatherstone Beck. Cross this

The legendary Wasdale Head Inn

at the 280m contour, and once on the N bank of the beck, ascend the spur that curves around to the NE, never far from the beck below, to reach the **Black Sail Pass**.

3 Here there is an intersection of paths on the pass. Ignore the path bisecting yours – which links Pillar to Kirk Fell – and also ignore the path SA into the Ennerdale valley. The remaining path heads half R; it is this last of these paths you need to take, and it heads off initially to the E and drops into a crossing of Sail Beck at the 480m contour below a rocky gully. Cross the beck and ascend gently on the far side as the path traverses below Kirkfell and **Boat How** crags.

4 The path curves gently to the R around the NE edge of Boat How Crags, crossing a small stream before arriving at Beckhead Tarn. There are many paths off in a variety of directions, many of them to climbers' crags such as Napes Needle. The best running route is to pass to the R of Beckhead Tarn and continue on the path leading S just to the L edge of Gable Beck.

5 Keep descending, and two paths converge at the 300m contour on the spur of Gavel Neese. Below you is the maze of stone walls built on the valley floor of Wasdale Head to clear grazing land for sheep; in some places these walls are well over 5m thick, and date back to Neolithic times when these ancient enclosures were first made. Keep with the smaller track on the R as it descends SW to cross Fogmire Beck close to **Burnthwaite Farm**. This beck is famed as a spawning ground for salmon and sea trout.

6 When you join the Moses Trod path next to the beck, turn R and follow it along the bank to the confluence of the Fogmire and Mosedale becks. Turn L and retrace your earlier steps back to the pub at **Wasdale Head** where you started.

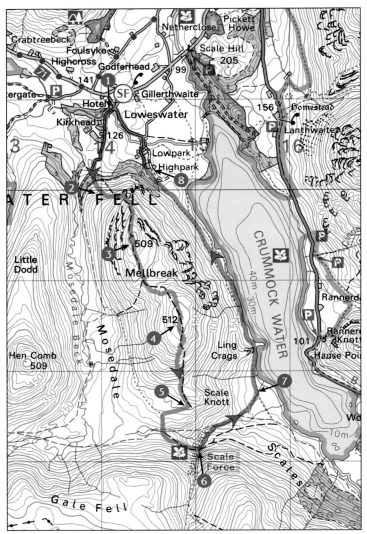

Route 25
Mellbreak and Crummock

Start/Finish	Kirkstile Inn, Loweswater
Distance	9.7km (6 miles)
Ascent/Descent	470m (1540ft)
Grade	Fell running, Level 3
Time	1hr 45min
High point	Mellbreak Fell (512m/1680ft)
Maps	1:25,000 OS Map OL4, 1:40,000 Harvey Lake District
Public transport	Bus 77/77A from Keswick
Parking	Ask in pub to use their car park

You can't visit the Kirkstile Inn without your eyes being drawn upwards by the craggy triangular shape of Mellbreak behind it. Its allure to a runner comprises a mix of fear and attraction to the aesthetic line that the ascent must take. After the climb the rewards are a visual overload, looking ahead down Crummock and Buttermere to Fleetwith Pike. Then there's a descent via the highest waterfall in the Lake District, and a return run along the shores of Crummock Water to a well-deserved pint at the end.

1 Turn R out of the pub, go past the church and immediately turn R at the crossroads down the lane signposted as a no through road, which curves around the back of the pub and continues on over the stone bridge across Park Beck. Run SA through a farmyard, where the road becomes a walled bridleway. About 300m beyond the farm there's a zig-zag in the tracks next to an ancient earthwork on the R, then after you pass through a gate, turn L and up through a small plantation onto open fellside.

2 The path keeps ascending, curving gently L and up the concavity of the slope. As the path steepens, it starts to zig-zag and the stone becomes looser underfoot, with increasing amounts of scree as you ascend. The route is easy to follow, as even without a

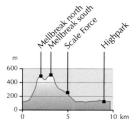

Mellbreak at the end of the Crummock valley

pitched path the line that countless pairs of boots have trod is evident, following the way of least resistance.

3. Pass two steeper pitches, and as the N ridge crest is gained you can look across Dropping Crag gully down to Crummock far below. Here the path veers S, then a short L traverse brings you up a rocky corner to regain the ridge above, where the difficulties are over as you climb the last few metres to reach the north felltop of **Mellbreak** at 509m. The south top is just 3m higher, with a saddle 40m lower between the two tops.

4. The south top affords the best views, which you should enjoy before dropping down the grassy slopes to the S – a delight to run down after the screes of the ascent and the heathers of the traverse.

5. When you reach the fence line, turn R and follow it until you join the path ascending from Mosedale, then turn L to descend 200m until you reach the bridleway that has come from the Floutern Pass route from Ennerdale foot. Instead of following the bridleway down to the L, run SA on a path that runs to the S of the fence line. This soon brings you to the edge of **Scale Beck**. Looking up the hillside you'll see a steep and wooded cleft; in the middle of this is the thin waterfall of the 40m drop of **Scale Force**.

6. After admiring the waterfall, follow the path down to the footbridge across Scale Beck and follow the main track down to rejoin the bridleway. Turn R to descend, and at the sheepfold where a path joins from the R, keep

contouring L to run down across the marshy alluvial fan of Scale Beck where it meets **Crummock Water**.

7 Run along the shores of Crummock, passing the peninsula of Low Ling Crag and then the islet of Iron Stone. After 300m, look for a faint track leading off to the L, which slowly parts from the lake to pass just above the first wall line below Dropping Crag. Follow it onwards below Green Wood and through **Highpark** Farm.

8 Continue SA along the lane and over Park Bridge, turning L on the far side. Run along the small road, and after 500m you'll see **Loweswater** church across the field ahead. The road brings you out at the small road junction next to the pub where you started.

Carry only what you need

The ascent on this route can be draining, and you should run with no more gear than you need. Consider cutting out the required section of map, or printing only that section, to avoid carrying a bulky full map. You could also coat it in Fablon for water resistance. Another lightweight tip is to waterproof electronic items with clingfilm rather than carry them in a bulky dry bag.

Route 26
Coledale Horseshoe

Start/Finish	Royal Oak pub, Braithwaite
Distance	13.8km (8½ miles)
Ascent/Descent	930m (3050ft)
Grade	Fell running, Level 3
Time	2hr 45min
High point	Eel Crag (Crag Hill) (839m/2753ft)
Maps	1:25,000 OS Map OL4, 1:40,000 Harvey Lake District
Public transport	Bus X5/77 from Keswick
Parking	Limited car park next to B5292 in Braithwaite

This route provides a great circuit of one of the lesser-visited of the valleys that radiate from Keswick. It is followed on a fell running race in April each year, takes in four Wainwright peaks, and is easy to access by car or public transport. The Coledale valley has a long history of mining, dating back to 1578, and the ores were rich in minerals including lead, silver, barium, zinc and cobalt. The Force Crag mine finally closed in 1990. This route loops around the fells of the far NW extremity of the national park – a fell runner's paradise with grassy ground underfoot and spectacular ridge lines. On this run you closely follow the route of the Coledale Horseshoe fell race.

1 Turn L out of the pub and run along the road through the narrows. Ignore the bridge over the beck and run SA, following the signposts to Whinlatter. Follow the road as it ascends, until you see a **car park** on the L and a stepped footpath ascending above the Whinlatter road. Ascend this and after 250m it doubles back on itself next to the plantation before climbing steadily up to the **Kinn** spur.

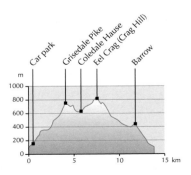

2 Here the running becomes easier as you follow the ridge towards the disused quarry at its end, before veering uphill on the rising traverse and rib of **Sleet How**, which brings you directly to the summit of **Grisedale Pike**. From here follow the ridge alongside the broken wall down to the SW to the head of **Hobcarton Crag**.

3 Continue SA at this point, ignoring the track that curves R along the crag headwall to Hopegill Head, and traverse the slopes around the head of Coledale Beck to reach the saddle of Coledale Hause ahead of you. While on the traverse you'll see the levels of Force Crag mine below you. (At this point, in the event of poor weather, you can turn L and descend on the Pudding Beck path past Force Crag mine, and along Coledale Beck to Braithwaite.)

4 At **Coledale Hause** there is a choice to make. Strong scramblers can run the racing line S up the steep rock steps of the north ridge of Eel Crag to reach its summit. Otherwise, for the recommended route, head SSW alongside Gasgale Gill to the path junction at 722m, where you turn L and straight up the path to reach the top of Eel Crag (shown as **Crag Hill** on OS maps).

Fell running down from Sail

5 Head down The Scar to the E, taking care on the couple of small rocky steps. From the col, head upwards to the top of **Sail**. (For those racing this route, it's possible to skirt around to the N of Sail to avoid the re-ascent, converging with the descent path to the ENE of the summit, at the path crossroads at 620m.)

6 Turn L and descend to the NE below the rocky outcrops on the NW aspect of Scar Crags, over **High Moss**, and at the path junction continue SA, ignoring the track off L over Outerside. Descend on the L bank of Stonycroft Gill, past the sheepfold to the S of Outerside, and run a further 300m before veering L on the small track that contours around above another sheepfold at the 400m contour, curving R above the valley head of Barrow Door and upwards to the top of **Barrow**.

7 Run SA down the NE ridge to reach Braithwaite Lodge at the fell foot, and follow the gated track N back into **Braithwaite**.

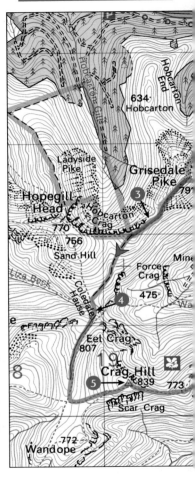

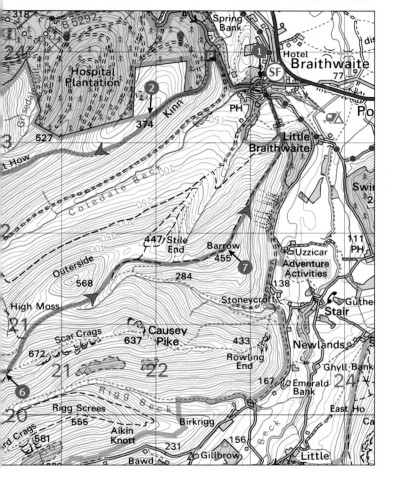

Route 27
Buttermere Sailbeck loop

Start/Finish	Bridge Hotel, Buttermere
Distance	15.4km (9½ miles)
Ascent/Descent	1135m (3725ft)
Grade	Fell running, Level 3
Time	3hr 10min
High point	Eel Crag (Crag Hill) (839m/2753ft)
Maps	1:25,000 OS Map OL4, 1:40,000 Harvey Lake District
Public transport	Bus 77/77A from Keswick
Parking	Car parking along road near pub

The Sail and Rigg becks occupy a quiet corner of the Lake District, with most walkers heading to the fells to the south of Buttermere, and drivers passing over Newlands Hause towards Keswick. This route really explores the central section of the Derwent fells, and is of particular interest to the fell runner as it involves good sections completely off-track, where judgement in reading the terrain is required to select the best running route. This loop follows the route of the Buttermere Sailbeck Horseshoe fell race.

1 Turn R out of the pub and head up the road past the village hall, and up the hill. As you pass the church, turn L up the road towards Newlands Hause, past the parking area on the L. Run up the road for 250m, at which point it kinks L then R to pass a farm building and water treatment works. Just 100m beyond this the fence veers L away

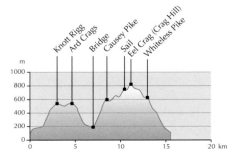

The church at Buttermere village

from the road, as does a thin path. Follow this as it contours around the hill-side between the road and Mill Beck.

2 Run along the edge of the beck for 1km, crossing Swinside Gill. On the far side of the beck, turn ENE up the gentle rounded spur that curves around to the L as you ascend. At the 450m contour you'll meet the walkers' track ascending from Newlands Hause; follow it upwards to the top of **Knott Rigg**.

3 Head along the ridge to the N then NE to reach a marshy col, before ascending the ridge ahead to **Ard Crags**. Follow the path onwards above **Rigg Screes**, after which it turns due E over the steeper step down **Aiken Knott** to the 320m contour, where a track heads off NE down to Rigg Beck and alongside it down to the small stone bridge and the road descending from Newlands Hause.

4 Cross the bridge, and immediately on the far side turn L onto the path along the N bank of Rigg Beck. Ahead you can see the triangular shape of Causey Pike dominating the view. Run for about 500m along the river track before turning R and ascending the fellside to reach the ridge at Sleet Hause. This

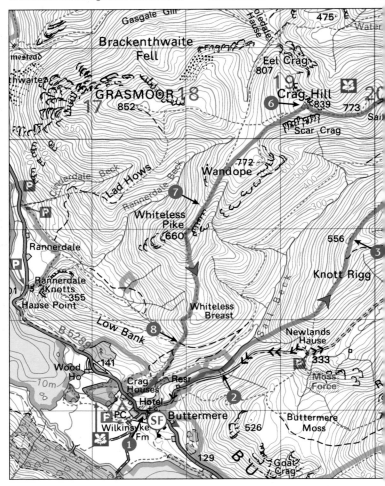

involves 250m of vertical and is tough on the legs, but there's a brief reprise as you turn L to follow the ridge towards **Causey Pike**, before the gradient steepens again to bring you to its summit.

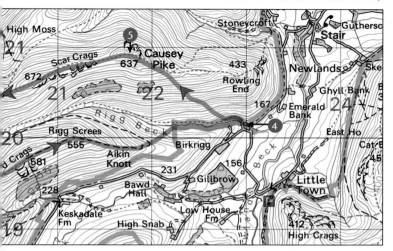

5   Run WSW along the ridge over **Scar Crags** and down to the Sail Pass, before a re-ascent to **Sail**. Here there is a steeper descent onto the ridgeline of The Scar, which leads upwards via two rock steps to the top of Eel Crag (shown as **Crag Hill** on OS maps), the highest point on this route at 839m.

6   Now there is a section of real fell running, where the fastest route choice doesn't follow a path. Head down the well-repaired track to the SW for 500m before ignoring the path that veers L to Wandope and running SA to contour across the middle of Wandope Moss in a SW direction to reach the top of Whiteless Edge ridge.

7   Run down this sharp ridge to reach Saddle Gate, and onwards up the slight ascent to **Whiteless Pike**. This marks your final fell top and the start of the long descent to Buttermere village. Turn to the S and follow the paths down over the top of **Whiteless Breast** before veering slightly R.

8   At the 300m contour you'll pass the top of the Rannerdale valley, and at the path junction soon after keep R, following the path down towards Grassgarth Copice and onto the road, where you turn L and continue to the end of the run in **Buttermere**.

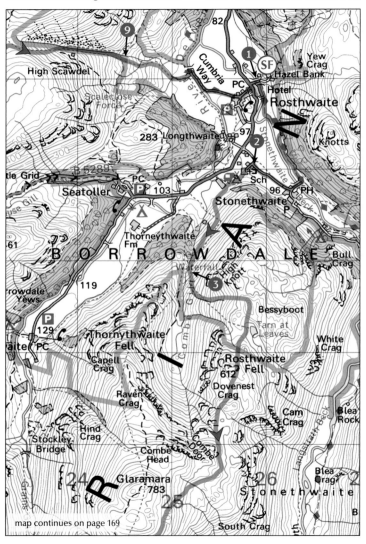

map continues on page 169

Route 28
Borrowdale loop

Start/Finish	Scafell Hotel, Rosthwaite
Distance	26.5km (16½ miles)
Ascent/Descent	1760m (5775ft)
Grade	Fell running, Level 4
Time	5hr 5min
High point	Scafell Pike (977m/3205ft)
Maps	1:25,000 OS Map OL4 and OL6, 1:40,000 Harvey Lake District
Public transport	Bus 78 from Keswick
Parking	Car park to L of B5289 beyond pub

You'll want to have had a good breakfast before taking on this loop, which includes the highest point in England and up to eight Wainwright fell tops. It follows the route of the tough Borrowdale fell race, held on the first Saturday of August each year. The record is still held by Billy Bland with an incredible time of 2hr 34m 38s, set in 1982. This might just be one of the hardest fell running records to beat, and may well stand for decades to come. The route includes several objectives that walking guidebooks give separate sections to, and there are four distinct massifs to cross: Glaramara, the Scafell group, the Gables and Dalehead.

1 Turn R out of the pub, and immediately after leaving the grounds turn R over a bridge across **Stonethwaite Beck**, turning R again on the far side to follow it upstream for 1km along the Cumbria Way path. Turn R to cross Stonethwaite bridge and run into the picturesque hamlet of **Stonethwaite**, turning R again along the road for 500m.

The route starts at the Scafell Hotel in Rosthwaite

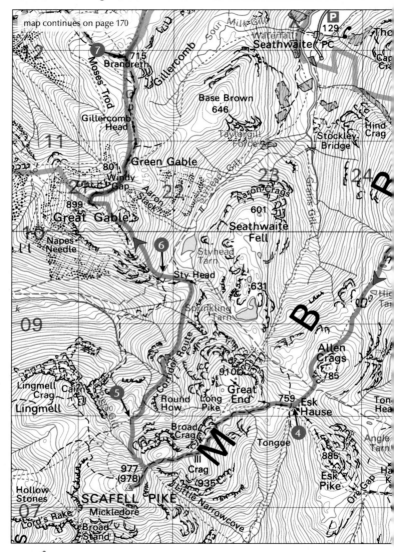

map continues on page 170

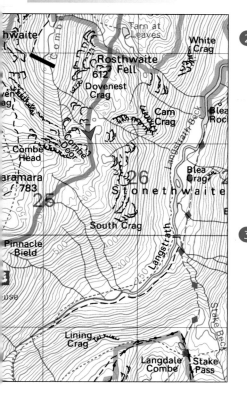

2 As you pass the **school**, turn L at the corner of the road and along the lane to the pretty white rendered church. Run through the farm along the footpath to the wall line above the **campsite**. Before you reach Combe Gill there's a L turn towards Rosthwaite Fell; follow this until you pass the last wall line, after which you soon reach Dry Gill beck.

3 Follow this up the fell-side, and when it runs out continue SA to reach **Bessyboot**. From here run due S past the **Tarn at Leaves** and onwards towards Great Hollow. Run for 2km in a SSW direction across a broken fellside of bogs, small tarns and out-crops. Pass Glaramara to the S to avoid extra height

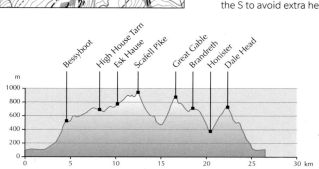

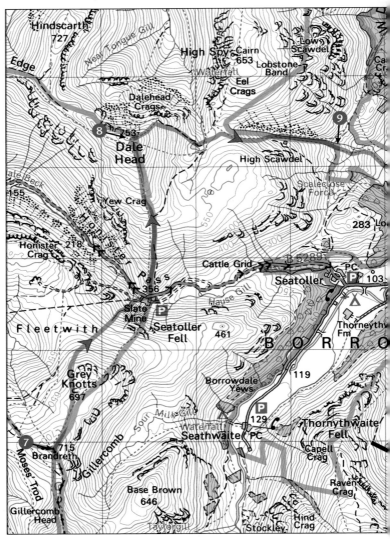

gain (or you can detour to its summit if you want to tick it off), traversing above Woof Gill and then Driedley Gill. You'll intersect the walkers' paths near **High House Tarn**, and can skirt around **Allen Crags** keeping them to your L, to arrive at **Esk Hause** (again, you could nip up to the summit of Allen Crags if you wish).

4 At Esk Hause, take the path heading W to traverse below **Great End** and ascend over increasingly rocky ground to pass **Broad Crag**. Here you descend to a col before making the last ascent up the ridge to reach the top of **Scafell Pike** (977m). You won't be alone up here! Take in the view, which is especially striking towards Great Gable and Styhead Tarn. Return to the col below Broad Crag and turn L to descend the path until you reach the **Corridor Route**.

5 Turn R and follow the Corridor Route along the contour path below Great End and Spouthead Crag, to the path junction with the Esk Hause track. Turn L and follow it to **Styhead Pass** and the mountain rescue stretcher box.

6 Ascend NW straight up the path to reach the summit of **Great Gable** before turning R and descending NE towards **Windy Gap**. This involves a few rock steps, so take particular care on a wet day when the rock is greasy. From the col, continue up over **Green Gable** and then N past the boundary posts along **Gillercomb Head** and its numerous tarns, and over the top of **Brandreth**.

7 The fastest route from here to Honister turns **Grey Knotts** and its outcrops to the W, before curving to the R before you reach the Drum House and descending to the road crossing at **Honister Pass**. Cross the road and head N up the hillside to reach **Dale Head**.

8 The next section descends E to pass by the foot of Dalehead Tarn, before cutting across open fellside ENE to contour around into the head of Tongue Gill and intersect the path leading down through the old Rigghead

Quarries. Follow the path down past the climbing hut, going SA as you cross the Allerdale Ramble path that cuts across at the 200m contour.

9 Continue following the path down until you reach the footbridge and the River Derwent in the valley floor. Turn L to cross the Derwent at New Bridge before running R along the bank on the Cumbria Way path and along the lane into **Rosthwaite**. Arrive at the road in a farmyard and turn R at the barn, then immediately L along a footpath, which after 200m arrives at the road directly in front of the hotel where you started.

Mixing it up

On a longer fell run such as this, try and make a conscious decision to alter your pace, to avoid getting into a monotonous trudge. This will increase your speed, concentration and motivation. One way to trigger a change in pace is to aim for certain ascent and descent rates (e.g. +15m/min when climbing, and -30m/min when running down). Another good technique is to imagine yourself consciously changing gears as though on a mountain bike, as you adapt to the terrain.

Route 29
Walla Crag and Castlerigg

Start/Finish	Dog & Gun pub, Keswick
Distance	10.6km (6½ miles)
Ascent/Descent	300m (985ft)
Grade	Trail running, Level 1
Time	1hr 40min
High point	Walla Crag (379m/1243ft)
Maps	1:25,000 OS Map OL4, 1:40,000 Harvey Lake District
Public transport	Multiple bus connections from Windermere and Penrith
Parking	Pay & display parking in Keswick

Many of the routes in this book assume you have a day or several hours to spare for a run. This one is shorter, and an ideal option for those staying in Keswick who have less time to spare. It starts and ends in the centre of the town and explores some of the best sights: the shores of Derwent Water, Walla Crag, and the ancient stone circle of Castlerigg. Despite the modest height gains, this run has great views and is a perfect choice for poor weather days, or in the winter months even in the snow.

1 Turn R out of the pub. To your L is Moot Hall, the start and finish point for all Bob Graham Rounds, but you turn R and run along the pedestrian street until you reach the George Fisher outdoor store. Turn R and run down Lake Road in front of the shop, and veer L through the subway under the main road. On the far side, around the edge of Hope Park,

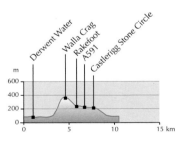

you can follow Lake Road onwards and past the **car park** until you reach **Derwent Water**. Ahead of all the boat landing stages you can see Derwent Isle and Catbells beyond.

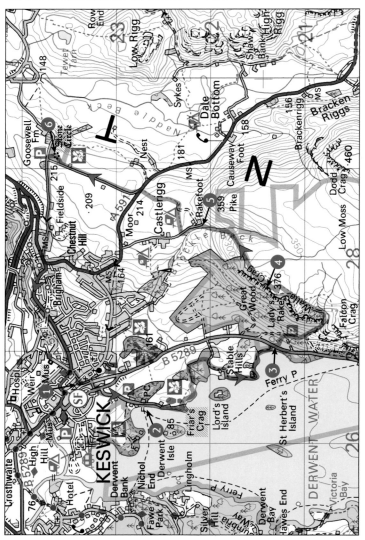

2 Run along the promenade beside the lakeshore to **Friars Crag**, where you'll see the Ruskin memorial on the mount. Pass the small rocky outcrop and descend the steps. Go through the gate and R to follow the path along the shore. At the next gate follow the path along the marshy edge of the woods of The Ings. Bear R and cross the footbridge to continue around the woodland to reach a farm track. Turn R and run along the track to **Stable Hills** Farm. Keep following the footpath signs and it will bring you around to the lakeshore once more, and past Broomhill Point into Calfclose Bay. Here you may have to dodge photographers trying to capture images of the Centenary Stone in the reflections on Derwent Water. Continue around and over the footbridge, and then after 100m turn sharp L to reach the main road. Cross this and go over the wall on the far side onto a footpath.

3 The path heads R then L to cross the **car park** road. Continue SA and turn R on the track, which tapers to a path to reach Cat Gill and ascends just above the beck. Follow the path upwards, climbing steeply before emerging above the treeline onto the open fell. Use the wall on your L as a navigational handrail, running along it and over the rock step-stile over the wall before heading directly for the summit.

The Centenary Stone in Derwent Water

Castlerigg stone circle above Keswick

4. From the top of **Walla Crag**, pass the cairn and veer R to cross the wall by a stone step-stile. Turn L and run down the slope, turning the marshy section ahead to the R. The path gets more obvious and turns into a track. Run along this until you reach the farm at **Rakefoot**. Continue down to the gate and through it, crossing the beck on the footbridge to reach the road.

5. Turn L down the road and follow it for 150m until you see a gate on the R signposted to the stone circle. Run along the track across the fields to reach the crossing of the **A591 road** at Nest Brow. Take extra care with this road crossing, as cars travel too fast on this section. Take the small road called Castle Lane on the far side and run along it for 1km, after which a stone step-stile on the R gives you access into the Castlerigg Stone Circle field.

6. Take in the views before exiting via one of the gates on the N edge of the field. Turn L down the road and follow it for just over 1km to reach the A591 again. Turn R and follow it back into **Keswick**. When you reach the war memorial, turn L onto Station Street and follow it upwards until it turns sharp L next to The Royal Oak pub. Turn R here and you can see Moot Hall ahead of you, and the pub where you started.

Route 30
Skiddaw

Start/Finish	The Sun Inn, Bassenthwaite
Distance	20.6km (12¾ miles)
Ascent/Descent	1085m (3560ft)
Grade	Fell running, Level 3
Time	3hr 50min
High point	Skiddaw (931m/3054ft)
Maps	1:25,000 OS Map OL4, 1:40,000 Harvey Lake District
Public transport	Bus 73 from Keswick
Parking	Car parking along road near pub

Skiddaw dominates the horizon north of Keswick, yet to run it on the Bob Graham Round route directly up from Moot Hall is a long slog, and often the short end to an ill-planned round. The northerly aspects of the mountain are far from monotonous, and this route is a nice mixture of well-established trails, including sections of the Allerdale Ramble and Cumbria Way, as well as true fell running across open mountainside where route choice is open to interpretation. Of appeal to fell runners is that there is a variety of terrain, and the fell running is easy underfoot on open expansive slopes. This makes it an ideal choice for those seeking an easier fell run in terms of terrain and route-finding, with panoramic views as a reward.

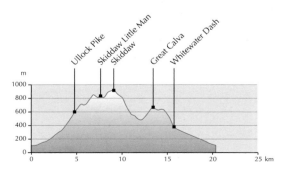

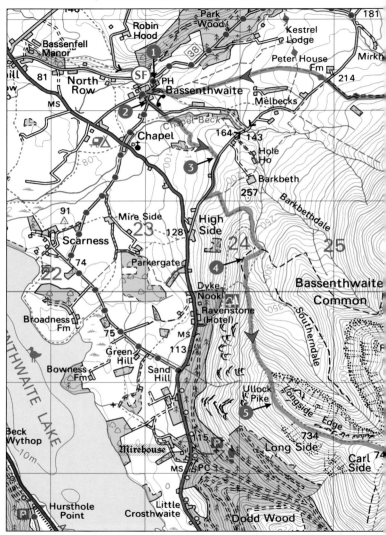

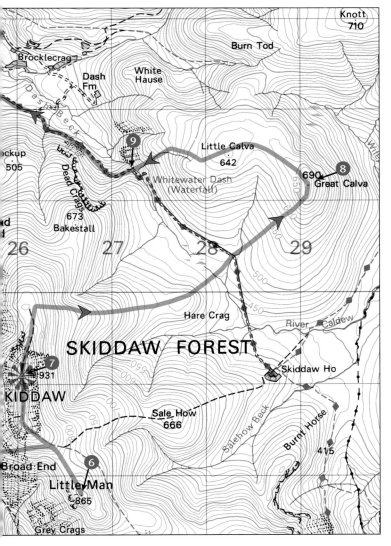

Skiddaw and Little Man above Keswick

1. Run directly down the road in front of the pub and veer L when you reach the village green, next to the red post box. Run along the road through the green, and at the end opposite the farm buildings, turn L again. At the junction just beyond, keep L and run along the hedged lane. You'll have great views of Ullock Pike and Skiddaw ahead of you.

2. Where the lane turns sharp L, run SA over the stone stile and across the field, then across the footbridge over **Chapel Beck**. On the far bank, follow the path L and cross another stile. Run along with the hedgerow on your L, following the path for 600m across the fields, with a final diagonal section to the stile onto the road next to a seven-bar gate.

3. Turn R and run along the road past High Side House, and onwards the same distance again. This brings you to a layby with a gate and stile on its near edge. Go over the stile and follow the bridleway up L towards Barkbeth for 200m beyond the small beck, before turning R. Run over a series of stiles over the wall lines to emerge above the walls onto the open fell. Ahead lies the obvious ridgeline, and the path cuts L across it before veering R to gain the rock outcrops of The Watches.

4. Run S up the ridge over the series of small outcrops of Ling How, where a path joins from the R, and then Kiln Potts. Ahead the ridge sharpens over The Edge before a steeper haul up to **Ullock Pike**. There's been significant path erosion on the softer ground here, so ensure you stick to the path created by the Fix the Fells teams to avoid further damage.

5. Run SA along **Longside Edge** and up to the top of **Carl Side**, where you turn NE to drop down to the tiny Carlside Tarn. Here you can avoid the worst of the screes by running E across the open fellside to the L edge of the saddle between Little Man and Skiddaw. You'll be running on scree that is stable underfoot, but there's no track, so keep on a bearing of 85 degrees in poor visibility, so as not to drift onto the steeper ground dropping into Broad End and Tongues Beck Head. Continue until you reach the fence line and turn R to take in the summit of **Little Man**.

6. Retrace your steps in a NW direction and run SA beyond the fence corner, where the Bob Graham Round route ascends to join from the R, to ascend the S end of Skiddaw's broad summit ridge. The slate scree underfoot has been used to create a couple of wind shelters, and the top is marked by the **trig pillar**.

7. Run N for 700m to a saddle, with the ring contour of the 831m spot-height ahead of you. Turn R to cross the fence and run down the spur of Blake Hill to Hare Crag. Initially there is a small path, which joins a quad bike track; where this descends to the L, run SA over **Hare Crag** on the path and follow it to the intersection with the Skiddaw House track at a small bridge over Dead Beck. Using the beck as a handrail, follow its S bank for 200m before veering R to run NE directly up to the top of **Great Calva**.

8. Here the Bob Graham Round route heads SE, but you turn L and run NW along the fence line to the top of the rarely visited **Little Calva**. Here the fence has turned in a SW direction; follow it to its corner and SA down the marshy hillside until you reach Dash Beck and the Skiddaw House track again. Turn R and run along the track, passing the waterfall of **Whitewater Dash**.

9. The last section of the run is straightforward, as you continue along the well-marked Cumbria Way track down through the bowl below **Dead Crags**. As you pass the fell wall line you meet a farm track; veer L to follow it to the road junction at **Peter House Farm**. Cross the road and follow the bridleway

Running on Skiddaw in winter conditions

diagonally L across the field to then go along the fence line through a series of gates in a W direction. The bridleway is evident, and gives way to a lane that brings you out into **Bassenthwaite** village centre opposite the red post box you ran past earlier. Turn R and retrace your steps along the road back to the pub.

Do the maths and keep warm

Skiddaw can be a very cold place. As a rough calculation, you will lose one degree centigrade every 100m that you ascend, so always look at the high point on any run to ensure you carry enough clothing. The MWIS and Met Office websites provide mountain forecasts that tell you the freezing levels and wind speeds, as well as their effect on you. As a rough idea, most runners find it impossible to make forward progress when the wind is gusting over 70km/h. You need to keep warm, and adapt plans if necessary.

NORTH-EAST LAKES

Runner at dawn on Blencathra (Route 31)

Route 31
Blencathra loop

Start/Finish	Horse and Farrier pub, Threlkeld
Distance	13.8km (8½ miles)
Ascent/Descent	735m (2410ft)
Grade	Fell running, Level 4 (with a section of skyrunning Level 4 on Sharp Edge)
Time	2hr 30min
High point	Blencathra (868m/2848ft)
Maps	1:25,000 OS Map OL5 and OL4, 1:40,000 Harvey Lake District
Public transport	Bus X5 from Keswick
Parking	Car parking along road near pub
Warning	Due to the skyrunning section on Sharp Edge, this route should only be attempted in dry weather and by those with a good head for heights.

The mountain of Blencathra, or Saddleback as it was originally known, is the most stunning peak you see when driving along the A66 into the Lake District, taking in the tantalising view of Sharp Edge and the huge buttresses of Doddick, Halls, and Gategill Fells rising suddenly upwards from the floodplains. Blencathra is a mighty fell, almost a massif in its own right, so distinct it is geologically from the Skiddaw group to the west. This route involves some skyrunning along Sharp Edge, and wild open fell running on the descent back to Threlkeld.

1 Turn R out of the pub and run along the road until you cross the Kilnhow Beck just before the church. On the far side of the bridge turn sharp R and follow the footpath sign up the lane. After 100m look out for a turn-off to the R to cross the beck again. The footpath crosses the fields on a series of diagonal traverses. After 750m you arrive at **Gategill** Farm; run into the farmyard and turn L onto the bridleway that leads onto the fellside. Turn R and cross the Gate Gill stream, then contour along the hillside with the wall on your R side.

Blencathra viewed from Castlerigg

2 After 1km you'll cross **Doddick Gill**, then after another 750m Scaley Beck. Keep running along the wall until you see a path contouring around to the west-facing slopes of Scales Fell. Here, climb around the W edge of the bowl of **Mouthwaite Comb** before rounding the corner to head NW above the valley of the **River Glenderamackin**. As you pass the 500m contour the path veers L to reach Scales Beck; cross the beck and follow the N bank towards **Scales Tarn**.

3 Here the path veers NNW to ascend towards **Sharp Edge**, before curving L as the crest is reached.**Only contemplate the following section if the rock is dry and you have a good head for heights**. Run along the ridge and on the upper section it becomes narrow, although the rock is generally sound for slate. The crux of the route is the

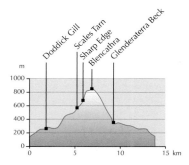

185

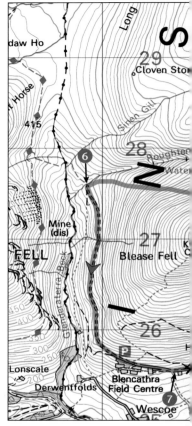

short section across the slabs and delicate moves of the Postbox. If it's too wet to safely contemplate Sharp Edge, turn around and run back down Scales Beck to the 520m contour, then turn L and run along the path below Brunt Knott, to reach the NE ridge of Atkinson Pike. Here you turn L and follow the ridge to the summit at 845m, at the top of Sharp Edge.

4 The difficulties are soon passed (the scrambling and skyrunning section is only 300m long) and you top out on Atkinson Pike. Turn L to head S up the easier slopes to reach the summit of **Blencathra** (868m). Enjoy the views – all the technical sections are behind you and there's a nice section of fell running ahead of you.

5 Rather than following the ridge crest to the SW, head W across the open fellside above Roughten Gill for just over 2km, aiming for the sheepfolds and ford of the bridleway at the 330m contour. There's a series of sheep tracks and open fell to follow, and the descent is low gradient, so it's easy on the legs.

6 When you reach the bridleway, turn L and follow it S down the beautiful **Glenderaterra Beck**. As you finally reach the wall line the track curves L around the spur of Blease Fell to reach the road head at the small **car park** above the field studies centre. Run SA along the road to the cattle grid then take the small path on the L along the fence line, running parallel with the road.

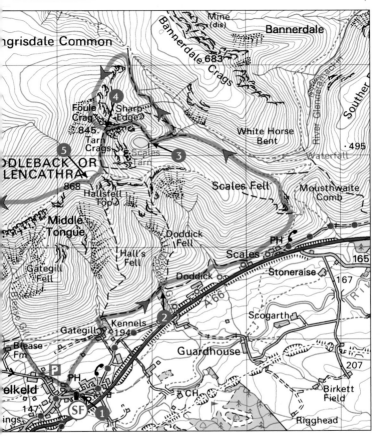

7 The path passes through a series of gates and goes through **High Row Farm** before contouring away from the road to **Blease Farm**. Another 150m brings you to **Blease Gill**, where you turn sharp R to follow the path down the edge of the beck and go through a small car park on the edge of **Threlkeld**. Continue alongside the beck and you'll soon recognise the path turn-off that you took earlier. Run SA and retrace your steps to reach the road, turning L to finish at the pub.

Route 32
Dockray coach road

Start/Finish	The Royal Hotel, Dockray
Distance	20.8km (13 miles)
Ascent/Descent	795m (2610ft)
Grade	Fell running, Level 2
Time	3hr 25min
High point	Stybarrow Dodd (843m/2766ft)
Maps	1:25,000 OS Map OL5, 1:40,000 Harvey Lake District
Public transport	Nearest bus is 508 to Aira Force, ½ mile S of start
Parking	Ask in pub to use their car park, or park at the end of the Old Coach road (Waypoint 2)

The Old Coach Road between Dockray and St Johns in the Vale is a former trade route across the northern foothills of the Helvellyn range. This run follows the coach road and makes a traverse over the upper section of the range. There's an even split of pure trail running and fell running on open grassy fellside, where the runners' route differs from that of the walkers. The navigation is straightforward, and the rounded mountains of this area of the range mean there's little steep or craggy ground to negotiate. Between Clough Head and Stybarrow Dodd, you closely follow a section of the Lakes in a Day race route, and part of the Bob Graham Round.

1 Coming out of the pub you stand at the road junction; turn R and follow the signpost up the small road towards High Row and Dowthwaite Head. Run along the road, soon leaving the hamlet and farm buildings of Dockray behind and venturing into pretty rolling countryside. After nearly 2km you'll arrive at a road junction; run SA across the road to join the Old Coach Road.

2 Run along the Old Coach Road with **Cockley Moor** forest to your R, and after 700m turn R to head N and reach **Groove Beck**. There's a ford for horses, 4x4 vehicles and bikes, or a footbridge so you can keep your feet dry.

3 After a further 3km of running – during which the track borders marshy moorland and you pass the bogs of Sandbed's Moss and Wolfcrag Moss,

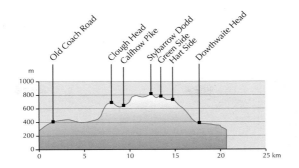

while the ground N of the track is the open rolling moorland of Threlkeld Common – you'll come to Mariel Bridge over Mosedale Beck. Continue following the Old Coach Road in a NW direction.

4   The track rounds the E spur of White Pike; run for another 800m until it starts to descend ahead of you, on the apex of the N spur of White Pike. Here on the L is a stile, which you cross to run up the hillside, heading S. After ascending 200m the gradient starts to ease, and you reach a boulder field on the final section of the slope.

5   From the cairn of **White Pike**, head SW towards the grassy block of **Clough Head**. It's always worth looking down to the R, at the scale of the huge landslip that caused the terminal debris mound of Threldkeld Knotts below. You also get a great view N of Blencathra and of Route 31.

Clough Head and the Dodds

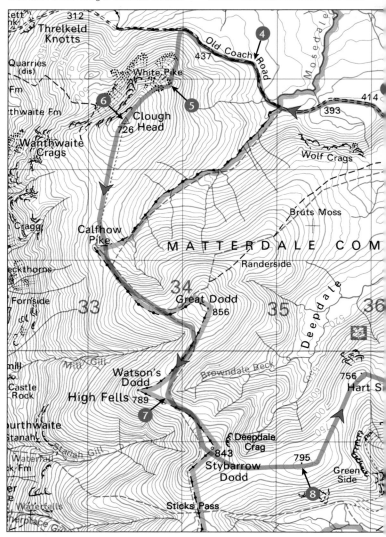

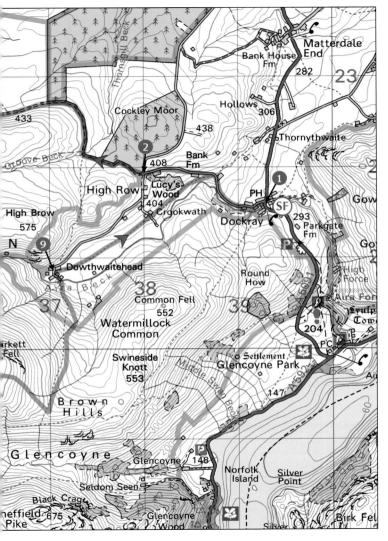

6 Run S over wonderfully grassy ground on the wide shoulder above the Mosedale Beck valley. Pass to the L of the subsidiary summit of **Calfhow Pike**, and curve gently L towards Great Dodd. For peak baggers, **Great Dodd** is a Wainwright fell top, but fell runners will spot a contour track at 790m that cuts across the top of Millgill Head and bypasses the top of Great Dodd. The paths converge on the saddle between Great and Watson's Dodd.

7 **Watson's Dodd** can similarly be turned to the L side, but the Wainwright collectors may wish to pay a visit to its top. Continue SE to reach the summit of **Stybarrow Dodd**, which is the most southerly Dodd of the Helvellyn range. From here, continue SA in the same direction for 250m to reach the marshy saddle with Green Side, and veer L to head E and reach **Green Side** with its collection of cairns.

8 Now follow the ridgeline around to the L, heading NNE along the obvious spur to reach **Hart Side**, then veer R to head E to the minor top of **Birkett Fell**. This point offers stunning views down to Ullswater, and of the Helvellyn range. Turn R and follow the wall for 700m until you reach a path, where you turn L and descend over increasingly marshy ground to cross the footbridge over Aira Beck and into the **Dowthwaite Head** farm buildings.

9 Before you reach the road there's a footpath off to the R across the fields, which you run along via **Crookwath** Farm. Continue along it for 2km and you'll pass into some woodland shortly before arriving at the road on a corner. Turn R and retrace the first 600m of your run back to the pub buildings at **Dockray**.

Pole art

There's plenty of scope for using poles on this route. On steep grassy slopes you can plant your downhill pole and brace your foot against it for extra traction. This technique also works on scree or mud. Most runners find the greatest benefits of poles when ascending steep slopes. With a little practice poles will make a climb aerobically easier thanks to improved efficiency gained through better posture and splitting the load through different muscle groups.

Route 33
Gowbarrow loop

Start/Finish	Brackenrigg Inn, Watermillock
Distance	15.8km (9¾ miles)
Ascent/Descent	525m (1720ft)
Grade	Trail running, Level 2
Time	2hr 30min
High point	Gowbarrow Fell (481m/1578ft)
Maps	1:25,000 OS Map OL5, 1:40,000 Harvey Lake District
Public transport	Bus 508 from Windermere/Penrith
Parking	Ask in pub to use their car park, or use Aira Force car park (NY400199) near Waypoint 6.

This is a great loop if you're after a trail running route with good views that doesn't venture too high. It's an ideal choice for one of those days when the cloud base is quite low but you want to get out anyway. It's perfect as an evening run, as you can watch the sun cast its long shadows over Ullswater, before descending for a pint at the end as a reward. This route follows a section of the new Ullswater Way footpath, which is well signposted and maintained, so it's ideal if your navigational skills aren't strong.

1 Turn R out of the pub and immediately R again down the small side-road. Run away from Ullswater, along the road for 1km to reach the village of **Bennethead**. The road curves L; at the junction run SA, signposted towards Matterdale. After 100m the road curves gently R, and just after a couple of mature trees on the L is a wooden gate giving access to a well-signposted footpath.

2 Follow the path on a diagonal across the first couple of fields to reach Longthwaite Beck, then ignore the turn-off

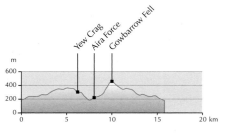

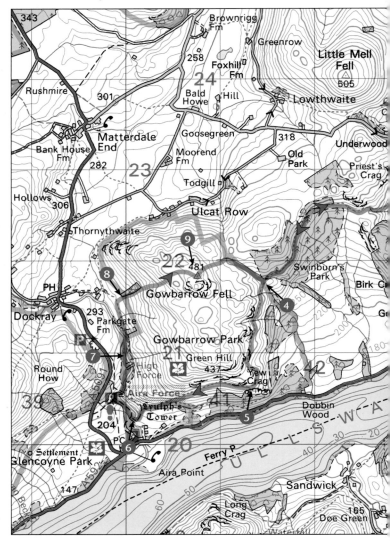

S to High Longthwaite and run SA in a SW direction over five more fields to reach a wooden gate through the wall onto the road.

3 Across the road is another gate, giving access to the footpath to Priest's Crag, which lies in front of you. Run along the track as it skirts around to the SE edge of the fellside, and from its S edge contour around and follow the path up the N bank of the beck, to then cross it and follow the path through and along the wall to its corner before heading SA along to the N edge of the woodland. The path then enters the woods and contours around to bring you out on the SW corner. Cross the small beck, then the open ground and a wall, to meet another path at the ruins of a shooting lodge.

4 Turn L and run S along the path, contouring up increasingly steep ground, on the E flanks of Gowbarrow. Follow the undulating path, with views ahead down to Ullswater, to reach its S end at the brow marked by a cairn. Go through the new gate to see the amazing view of the lake from the top of **Yew Crag** before retracing your steps to the gate and turning L to follow the track.

Save it for later

If your route involves running through forest – such as this one does on the approach to Gowbarrow – it's often best to avoid the early mornings when the exposed tree roots are covered with dew and especially slippery. Wait for the evening, when this route in particular comes into its own. Slopes with an E and S aspect dry fastest with the morning sun. Slopes with a W aspect often don't dry out until the afternoon, and N aspects can stay wetter, cooler and more slippery throughout the day.

5 Follow the path W along the steeper ground, past the memorial seat, and down the descent below Hind Crag. Across the field below you is **Lyulph's Tower**, an 18th-century hunting lodge that looks like a castle. Keep on running, and as you reach the woodland the path splits. Take the L fork to descend through the gate and down a steeper path into the section of forest called the Pinetum. Ensure you cross the beck via one of the footbridges to reach the W bank.

Looking down Aira Force from the bridge

6 Turn R and follow the well-defined paths up along Aira Beck to arrive below **Aira Force** waterfall, with the bridge across its head. You won't be the first to take a photo from this point, but it's hard to resist. Ascend the path up to the bridge and follow the beck on the path on the W bank. The path is quite rough in places, but there have been some repairs.

View across Ullswater from Gowbarrow

7 About 500m beyond Aira Force a path joins from the L; cross Aira Beck by the bridge to reach the obvious wall on the far side. Go through the gap and follow the signpost towards Dockray, running across two fields of open farmland. Before you reach the next gate in the wall, turn R and head up the hillside to the fell gate.

8 Cross this and run up the fellside, keeping the wall on your L. The path is pitched, and as you climb you pass from bracken to heather covering the ground. Ahead the trig point comes into view, and the ground becomes peaty underfoot, but the track is well maintained so you should keep your feet dry.

9 The views from the summit of **Gowbarrow** are worth a breather before you continue along the track, which descends and curves around to the R to reach the ruined shooting lodge you passed earlier. Turn L here and retrace your earlier route back to the pub.

Route 34
Askham and Patterdale

Start/Finish	Punchbowl Inn, Askham
Distance	33km (20½ miles)
Ascent/Descent	760m (2495ft)
Grade	Trail running, Level 2
Time	4hr 50min
High point	Chapel-in-the-Hause (399m/1309ft)
Maps	1:25,000 OS Map OL5, 1:40,000 Harvey Lake District
Public transport	Bus 106/111 from Penrith
Parking	Car parking along road near pub

This run follows a section of the Ullswater Way route as well as taking in some great moorland trails on easy terrain. It's a fantastic introduction to the southern edge of Ullswater, which is far less visited than the Glenridding and Pooley Bridge extremities. The ease of navigation over the moorland near the Cockpit Stone Circle has been much improved by the waymarking of the Ullswater Way, so this is a simple route to follow. The stone circle itself is thought to date to 2000BC. You start and end this route in the village of Askham, which sits just across the river from Lowther Castle. The outward section of the route can be combined with Route 39 and retraced back to Askham to follow the full route of the Tour of Helvellyn.

1 Turn L out of the pub onto the road that leads across the pretty village green. You'll arrive at a junction next to the village store, and a red telephone box, before a slight kink R and then L opposite the Queens Head pub take you onto the upper section of the green. Take the R-hand road, which is signposted as a dead end, and follow it up to its end next to the moor gate and a parking area next to the wall.

2 Run SA, ignoring the path splits off to the L. Keep running alongside the wall and after 1km you'll reach the wall edge at the small wood of **Riggingleys Top**. Run W for 600m to the next strip of woodland, and just before it turn half L to head SW. The track is good for a while, before tapering slightly to a narrower path, bringing you to the stone circle of **The Cockpit**.

Silver Hill and the Ullswater Way trail

3 Here High Street paths join from the N and S, but run SA to the W to contour around the hillside. Just beyond the Cockpit is a small ford, and you run
along the track for 1km to reach the intake wall next to the stream crossing
of **Aik Beck**. Run along the edge of the wall, and when it drops away below
you, keep following the bridleway path below the steep ground of Long
Crag and Auterstone Crag, to rejoin the wall line.

4 Run along the intake wall past **Swarthbeck**, enjoying the views of Ullswater
ahead of you. As you round the spur of Hewthwaite to enter Howtown Bay,

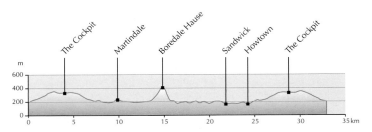

🏃 199

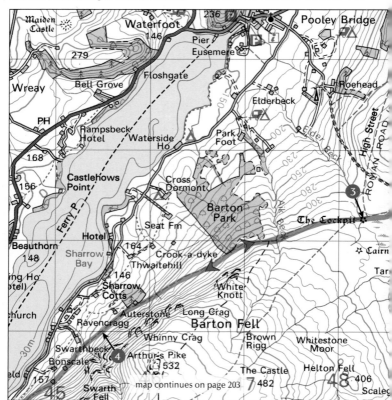

follow the bridleway contouring around to the S to reach the buildings at **Mellguards**, where it turns R to cross the Fusedale Beck by a bridge.

5. Run SA around the foot of the ridge of Steel End and follow the bridleway up The Coombs until you see the small church of St Peter in **Martindale** below you. Run down past the church to reach the road and turn L to follow it down, keeping R at the junction, to cross the stone bridge across Howegrain Beck.

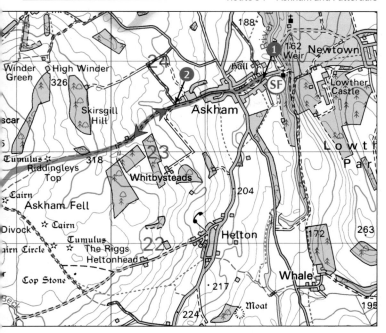

6 Follow the road around the spur and into Boredale and continue for 2.5km to the road end at **Boredale Head**. Here the bridleway continues SA to ascend above the intake wall towards **Boredale Hause**. The track steepens just before the col, and there's a lot of loose stone and scree underfoot.

7 At the pass, run SA and the paths turn NW to descend to Side Farm. Here turn R to follow the wall along the bridleway, heading N along the well-marked Ullswater Way path. Follow it for 2km, running close to the lake next to **Silver Crag** before curving around it to the R and into the mature woodland below **Birk Fell**. Run on the lake path through the woods and out the far side past Scalehow Force waterfalls, following the intake wall to reach the village of **Sandwick**. Cross the bridge and follow the footpath around to the L, then across the fields into Hallinhag Wood.

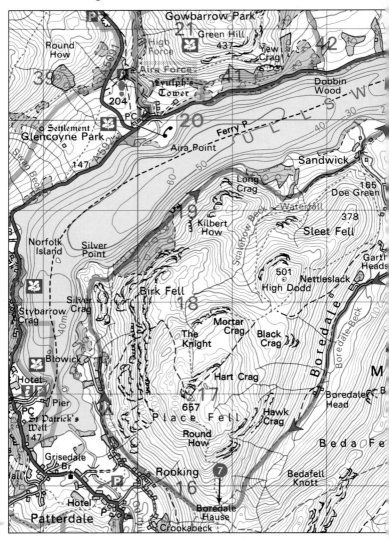

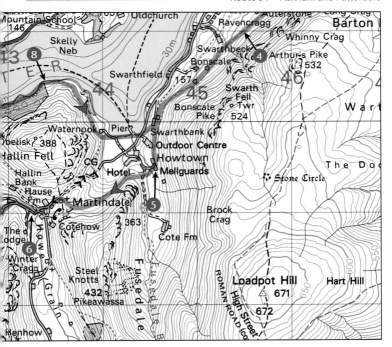

8　On the far side of the woods, round Geordie's Crag to turn SSE along the
wall line. At the buildings of **Waternook**, turn L down the footpath to the
lakeshore. Follow it past the pier and cross the road, then continue through
the gate to the L of the entrance to the **outdoor centre**. Follow the path
diagonally up the field towards the buildings in the top corner. There's a
gate to the R of the house gardens, which brings you out onto the bridleway
that you ran along earlier. Turn L and retrace your earlier route back to the
Cockpit and into **Askham**.

Route 35
Martindale circuit

Start/Finish	Howtown Hotel, Howtown
Distance	18.5km (11½ miles)
Ascent/Descent	825m (2705ft)
Grade	Fell running, Level 2
Time	3hr 10min
High point	High Raise (802m/2631ft)
Maps	1:25,000 OS Map OL5, 1:40,000 Harvey Lake District
Public transport	Bus 508 to Pooley Bridge, then ferry to Howtown
Parking	Ask in hotel to use their car park; some limited space just after the cattlegrid where the route leaves the road (Waypoint 1), or next to Martindale church (near Waypoint 9)

This route more than merits inclusion in this guidebook for two key reasons: firstly it explores a corner of the national park that is very rarely visited, following the skylines above Fusedale, Martindale, Bannerdale and Boredale, and secondly it's of historical interest as it follows a section of the old Roman road High Street from Red Crag to Rampsgill Head, and then a short section of the Coast to Coast path to Stoney Rigg. This run will get you away from the crowds and is a connoisseur's choice for great running in unspoiled scenery. Even on a bank holiday you'll normally have the majority of this circuit to yourself.

1 Turn R out of the hotel and run along the road through the narrows between the buildings. Run up the road, and at the junction keep R and continue SA and across the cattle grid. The ridgeline of Steel End is directly

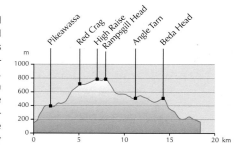

204

ahead of you; to access the ridge crest, turn R along the intake wall for about 100m towards a tree before taking a track off the L that ascends the ridge.

2 The path threads its way up through a series of outcrops, but it is not as steep as it first appears and the gradient eases. Follow the path as it curves gently S, and the summit is the rocky block of **Pikeawassa**. Below you to the L is the steep drop down into Fusedale, and to the R into Martindale and its deer forests. The deer herd are thought to originate from those that gave Hartsop village (to the SW) its name, translating as 'Valley of the Deer'.

3 Run down to the saddle ahead of you along the ridgeline and follow the wall line over Brownthwaite Crag traversing L to contour around **Gowk Hill** and crossing the marshy ground at the head of Fusedale before passing the ruins of a former shepherd's bothy next to a beck. Follow the wall up R for a short while before the path cuts up the hillside above the wall to reach the head of **Mere Beck**.

4 Follow the path upward to reach the ridgeline just N of **Red Crag**, where you turn S and follow the old Roman road of High Street onwards down to the marshy area of Redcrag Tarn. Run along the trail over **High Raise**, whose

Fell running on Beda Fell, Martindale

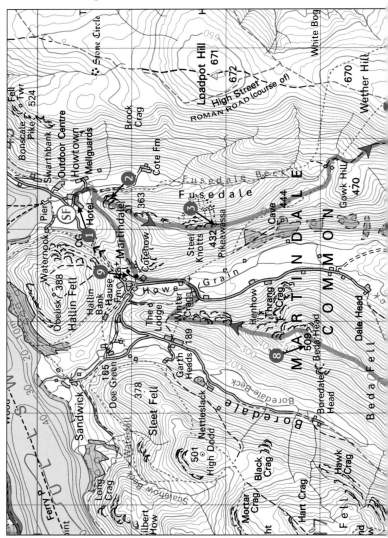

summit (802m) is marked with a cairn (the track passes to the W of the actual top, so a kink L is required for Wainwright collectors).

5 From High Raise, run down to a saddle with a tarn on it and ascend SA over the crest of **Rampsgill Head**, where the path drops SW to the wall line of the Straights of Riggindale. Turn R here and follow the path to skirt around the knoll of **The Knott**, and keep on the Coast to Coast path as it then dips down the slope to the L. Descend to the 600m contour, at which there is a path junction.

6 Take the R-hand fork in the track and run across the fellside to follow the path around the top of Prison Gill, then wind your way between the tiny tarns atop **Satura Crag** and follow the broad crest down to **Angle Tarn**, where you part company with the Coast to Coast path. At the tarn, look for a path cutting N towards Beda Fell. Make sure you don't take the R turn and descend into Bannerdale, as it is very steep and covered with scree.

7 The path N is grassy and wends its way past **Angletarn Pikes** above the steep ground of Heck Crags before slowly veering R to **Bedafell Knott**. There's a short descent, followed by a wonderful section of running over **Beda Fell** and **Beda Head**.

8 Here the descent starts, and you drop down over Howstead Brow and **Winter Crag** before reaching a path junction. Turn R and descend to Winter Crag Farm and the road. Turn L and run over Christy Bridge and past the tiny Old Church of St Martin. A further 300m along the road you'll spot a path off to the R, through a gate. Run along this gently rising track to the buildings at **Cotehow**. Immediately after this the path splits; keep R to follow the bridleway as it turns R to cut around the foot of Steel Knotts.

9 Pass Lanty Tarn and see Martindale church down to your L. Continue SA along the bridleway and in less than 1km you'll reach the intersection where you started your ascent of Steel Knotts earlier. Run SA to the road and turn L to retrace your initial steps back to the hotel in **Howtown** where you started.

Route 36
Patterdale loop

Start/Finish	Ramblers Bar, Inn on the Lake, Glenridding
Distance	14.5km (9 miles)
Ascent/Descent	190m (625ft)
Grade	Trail running, Level 1
Time	2hr
High point	Hartsop (217m/712ft)
Maps	1:25,000 OS Map OL5, 1:40,000 Harvey Lake District
Public transport	Bus 508 from Windermere/Penrith
Parking	Pay & display car park in Glenridding

This is a low-level route that is trail running in style. It is designed as a shorter route, and can be enjoyed if you only have a couple of hours to spare. The run starts and ends next to Ullswater and explores the whole length of the Patterdale valley. It provides a great training run, or an ideal choice if the weather in inclement or too wintery to venture into the higher fells.

1 Turn L out of the hotel grounds and cross the road to run along the footpath alongside the A592. Run past the Glenridding Hotel and shops, and after the buildings there's a footpath through the park on the L. When this reaches the boat hire centre next to the lake, turn R and cross the road to a footpath on the R of the road, which runs parallel to it until another road crossing just after a stone boathouse.

2 Run along the permitted path, and then pavement, as the road rounds a corner to the L in **Patterdale**, passing the fire station on the L and the church on the R. Continue until you see a sign for Side Farm, and turn L down the lane and follow it to the farm, which is nestled at the foot of **Place Fell**. Go through the farmyard and turn R to follow the bridleway for 200m until it

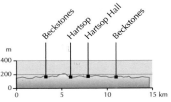

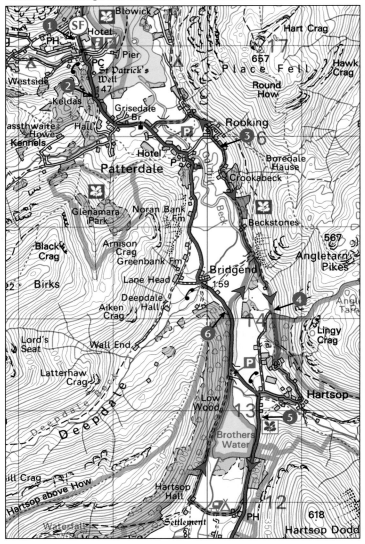

Side Farm and the flanks of Place Fell

joins a farm lane. Continue SA and at the cottages on the corner of the lane, run ahead onto the footpath, signposted to Hartsop.

3 Leave Rooking behind, and as you reach the next farm buildings, cross a stile on the L and then a small bridge on the permissive footpath to Hartsop. This rejoins the main footpath along a wide track. Follow it through **Beckstones** Farm, and at the split in the track, keep L on the bridleway. Run across Dubhow Beck, and after a further 300m reach Angletarn beck, where you take the L path and go through the gate in the wall.

Staying connected

Carry a mobile phone at all times when running. You can easily make it waterproof by wrapping it in cling film, through which it can still be used in the event of an emergency, or putting it in a resealable plastic freezer bag. This route is a good choice for wet days, so waterproofing your phone is all the more important. Always ensure you start your run with your phone fully charged, and to help protect its battery life on cold days carry it close to your body to keep it warm.

(4) At the next path junction, keep R and descend along the path to the first buildings of **Hartsop**. Follow the arrows to keep on the footpath, and once on the lane follow it down to a sharp R corner, where it becomes a proper road. Follow the road down to the junction with the **A592** and turn L to run along the road for 300m.

(5) On the R is a kissing gate giving access to the lakeshore; turn L and follow the permissive footpath to reach the Sykeside campsite. Veer R and cross the valley floor to **Hartsop Hall**, where you turn R onto the footpath alongside **Brothers Water**. At the **car park** at the far end, take the permissive footpath on the L and follow it alongside the road.

(6) When you reach a kissing gate, cross the road, and the stile on the far side. Follow the permissive footpath through the sparse woodland alongside Goldrill Beck, which you run along until you reach the bridge. Cross the stile and the bridge before turning L onto the bridleway. After 150m you'll reach the path junction you passed earlier; follow the signposted route back to **Patterdale** and retrace your earlier steps to return to **Glenridding**.

Route 37
High Street

Start/Finish	Brotherswater Inn, Sykeside
Distance	20.9km (13 miles)
Ascent/Descent	1200m (3935ft)
Grade	Fell running, Level 3
Time	3hr 50min
High point	High Street (828m/2717ft)
Maps	1:25,000 OS Map OL5 and OL7, 1:40,000 Harvey Lake District
Public transport	Bus 508 from Windermere/Penrith
Parking	Limited layby parking S of start on A592

This route is a great option for an early-morning or an evening circuit of the fells, when the Hartsop valley is in the shade and the long shadows of the mountains glimmer the golden colour of the bracken. On a good day, the vivid green of the pastures in the valley floor is in stark contrast to the blue skies, and the surfaces of Brothers Water and Hayeswater are calm mirrors drawing the eyes down from the fells and ridgelines. The route ascends six Wainwright summits, although a couple can be bypassed if you're looking to trim a few minutes off the circuit.

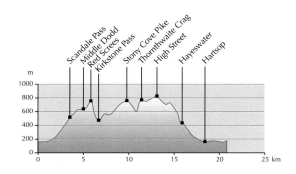

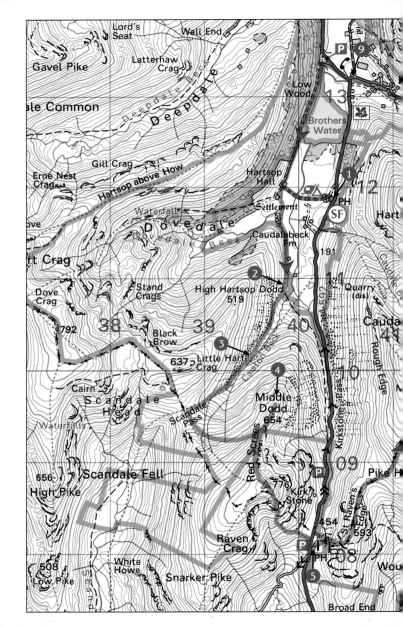

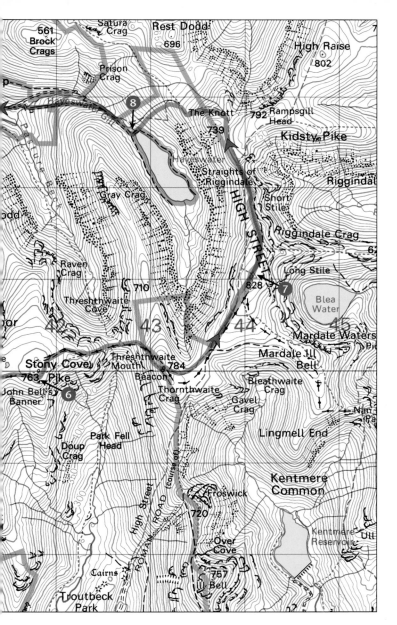

Middle Dodd with Patterdale beyond

1. Exit the pub into the car park, and next to the A592 you'll see a signpost indicating the footpath to Hartsop Hall. Run along the track past the **campsite** and across the bridge over Kirkstone Beck. At the **hall**, turn L and almost immediately L again to head S towards the Scandale Pass. This path leads across the fields to the base of **High Hartsop Dodd** and along the foot of its E aspect.

2. Run S alongside the wall, and at the junction at the 200m contour keep R to ascend beside **Caiston Beck**. Ignore the track off to the L across the footbridge, as this follows the road up to Kirkstone Pass. Continue ascending up the W bank of the beck, and at 260m the intake wall cuts away to the L. Now you are properly on the open fellside. The path is thin and braids its way up alongside the beck.

3. Just 500m beyond the intake wall you'll pass a disused level; look for its entrance on the L across the beck. A further 1km ahead, the gradient eases and you arrive at the marshy ground of the **Scandale Pass**. When you see the stile over the wall, turn L and contour E across the hillside in a rising curve to take in the summit of Middle Dodd. There are several outcrops to cross, but they are easily passed and you soon arrive on the grassy saddle near the corner of the stone wall on Smallthwaite Band.

4. It's worth taking in the summit of **Middle Dodd**, as the view N is spectacular, then turn around and run up the ridgeline to the top of **Red Screes**. Head SE, and as you reach the convex crest of the hillside you can see the Kirkstone Inn far below you. Run down the rocky path as it drops steeply down to the **car park** next to the pub.

5. Cross the road and follow the signpost to the L of the buildings, through the field with wind turbines to its top L corner, then run up the hillside next to the wall and up a rock step to reach the S end of **St Ravens Edge**. Turn L and run along the ridge, and follow the wall as it kinks R across a marshy section, re-ascending before heading up the broad spur of Caudale Moor. Follow the wall around to the R again to reach the top of **Stony Cove Pike**.

6. From the summit, run ENE to a track that descends some rocky steps, where a handhold may well be required, to reach the saddle of **Threshthwaite Mouth**. Continue SA and up the wall line ahead, zig-zagging up the screes before traversing R to come out at the beacon of **Thornthwaite Crag**. Run

Fell runner on Caudale Moor

E to join the obvious scar of the Roman road and follow it around to the L to reach the top of **High Street**.

7 Run N along the wall, and the ridge narrows to the **Straits of Riggindale**. Here, cross onto the R-hand side of the wall and ignore the turns to the R to Rampsgill Head, instead continuing SA to **The Knott**. Just beyond it the path drops off to the L; follow it down, keeping L at the junction. The view to Hayeswater below you is stunning, and any geographers will appreciate the swarm of drumlins and the alluvial fan, which seem straight out of a textbook.

8 The floods of December 2015 washed away the footbridge at the foot of **Hayeswater**, but it's possible to cross the stream further downstream, either by boulders or a footbridge. Once on the L bank of **Hayeswater Gill**, follow it down and just below the intake wall cross onto the N bank, to follow the path all the way into the village of **Hartsop**. You'll arrive at a small car park; follow the lane all the way to the main road next to a bus shelter.

9 Turn R and follow the **A592** for 300m to Cow Bridge and turn L into the car park, then L again onto the track to the W of **Brothers Water**. Run along this path down the length of the lake and onwards until you reach **Hartsop Hall**. Turn L and retrace your initial steps back to the pub where you started.

Route 38
Helvellyn skyline

Start/Finish	The White Lion pub, Patterdale
Distance	14.6km (9 miles)
Ascent/Descent	1025m (3365ft)
Grade	Fell running, Level 5 (with sections of Skyrunning, Level 3, on Striding Edge and Swirral Edge)
Time	3hr 5min
High point	Helvellyn (949m/3114ft)
Maps	1:25,000 OS Map OL5, 1:40,000 Harvey Lake District
Public transport	Bus 508 from Windermere/Penrith
Parking	Ask in pub to use their car park, or there are a few spaces in the layby next to the A592.
Warning	Don't be tempted to undertake this route if the weather is wet or icy, as the ridges become very slippery when wet.

This may not be a run for those seeking solitude, but for anyone who wants a challenge at the easy end of the skyrunning scale it's an ideal choice. Whilst described both as a hard fell run and easy skyrunning challenge, this route should not be underestimated, and very good mountain skills and sound judgment are required. The Helvellyn skyline route follows the mountain's two most famous ridges – Striding Edge and Swirral Edge – taking in the highest section of the Lakes Sky Ultra race route. Although the route features some erosion caused by countless visitors, runners can do their bit by sticking to the path to avoid further damage, and consider a donation to the Fix the Fells scheme.

1 Turn L out of the pub and cross the road into the pub car park on the far side. A footpath sign indicates the route up beside a row of cottages; behind the buildings turn R to follow the footpath across a footbridge and then L up the hillside. The path follows the intake wall for 600m to cross Hag Beck, then contours around the N end of Thornhow End before entering mature woodland. At the far side of the woods, cross the wall, and at the sheepfolds turn R and drop down to Thornhow Farm.

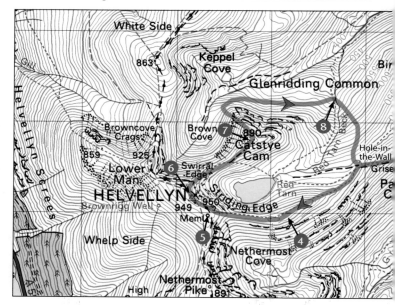

2 On the farm track, turn R then immediately L after the gate to cross the **Grisedale Beck**, and at the next corner continue SA across the field. At the intake wall, ignore the path following the wall line and turn L to cut next to the plantation on a rising traverse, heading W up the hillside.

3 There are two paths up the hillside which braid and rejoin at 480m, and again at the famous Hole-in-the-Wall. Here, turn L and run SW along the ridge crest above Bleaberry Crag. The path follows the N side of the ridge over Low Spying How, which marks the start of **Striding Edge**. Follow the ridge onwards to High Spying How.

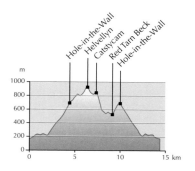

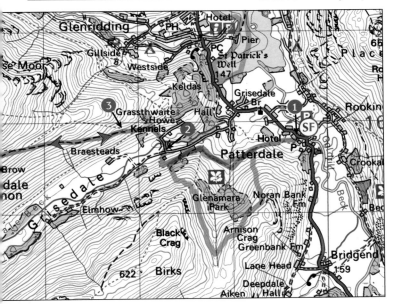

4 From High Spying How there's a short downclimb of a small chimney to a col. The ridge remains narrow and heads almost due W towards the bulk of Helvellyn. Down to your R the waters of Red Tarn sparkle. The best scrambling is on the ridge crest, but if the rock is slippery there's an easier path below most of the steeper sections. At its far end the ridge becomes less pronounced and you run up a scree-strewn path to the Charles Gough **memorial**. The legend goes that Gough died in a fall and his faithful dog remained with him for three months until it was discovered.

5 As you reach the **Helvellyn** summit plateau, turn R and follow the path up to the summit stone shelter and then NW for 100m to the trig point. Spare a thought for the fell-top assessors, who ascend each day of the winter season to report on conditions! Continue NNW for 100m and you'll see the descent route onto Swirral Edge.

6 Descend in a NE direction down the crest of **Swirral Edge**, keeping to the ridge top as much as possible. On several sections you'll need to use your

Runners on the summit of Helvellyn

hands, and after 500m you'll reach the col below **Catstye Cam**. Follow the path SA up to its summit.

7 Turn L and descend the NW ridge, keeping to the L side of the ridge as it's free of outcrops. This section is untracked fell running, where judgement is required in the choice of route. Drop down into Brown Cove and turn R, following the beck down to the old dam. Here you turn R again and follow the 550m contour across the lower slopes of Catstye Cam, below all the outcrops, until you reach **Red Tarn Beck**.

8 Run SSE in a rising traverse to reach the Hole-in-the-Wall on a re-ascent of 150m, and once there, retrace your earlier route back to the pub in **Patterdale**.

Keeping the stones out

When a route involves running over loose scree, consider wearing running gaiters to keep stones out of your shoes – or if wearing longer socks you can fold then down over the top of the shoes for the same effect. Gaiters and long socks are also useful for protecting your lower legs from cuts and grazes from sharp and abrasive rocks.

Route 39
Helvellyn tour

Start/Finish	The Traveller's Rest pub, Glenridding
Distance	25.3km (15¾ miles)
Ascent/Descent	1070m (3510ft)
Grade	Fell running, Level 2
Time	4hr 10min
High point	Sticks Pass (745m/2444ft)
Maps	1:25,000 OS Map OL5, 1:40,000 Harvey Lake District
Public transport	Bus 508 from Windermere/Penrith
Parking	Pay & display car park in Glenridding

This route is a great option when the weather is too poor, icy or windy for a safe ascent of Helvellyn, and it can be combined with the outward leg of Route 34 for a recce of the complete Tour of Helvellyn race route. There's much of interest, from the workings of the Greenside Mine to the barren stony desert of Sticks Gill and the ski tow on Raise on the first section. The traverse through the Thirlmere forests gives an insight into the level of destruction caused by the December 2015 storms, as you run above the reopened A591, which was variously washed away and covered by landslides. The second crossing of the range, passing Grisedale Tarn, follows a line of weakness via Raise Beck and down Grisedale.

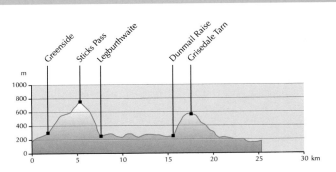

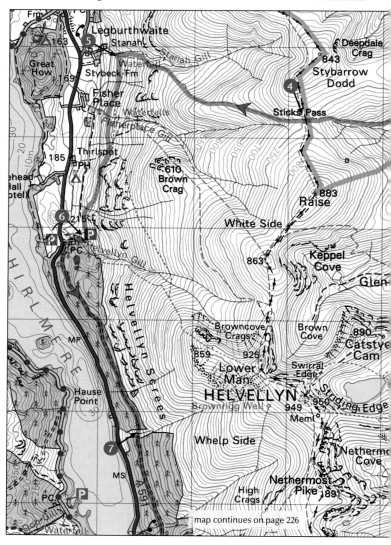

map continues on page 226

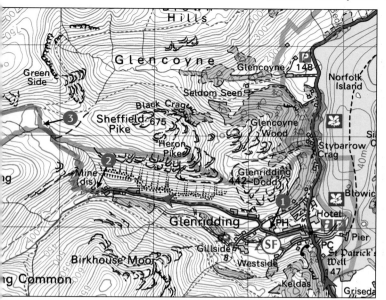

1. Turn R out of the pub and head up the Greenside Road, following a kink up R and then L, past a row of cottages. There should be no cars on this road, apart from residents'. Above you on the R are the Glenridding Screes; follow the road below them for 1.5km to reach the Helvellyn Youth Hostel below the junction with Swart Beck and the disused Greenside **mine buildings**.

2. Beyond the buildings, turn R up the zig-zags of the track, which is sign-posted to Sticks Pass. You'll gain height quickly on the initial section as you ascend below the crags of Stang End. Here the path rounds the steep ground to turn N then NW to the footbridge across Swart Beck.

3. Run along the path, which soon veers W to follow Sticks Gill (East) up to **Sticks Pass**. On your L is the ski tow on Raise, which always looks forlorn out of the snow. Run SA and follow the bridleway to the R bank of Sticks Gill (West). This section is open and exposed, so is often very windy; it's worth having a windproof jacket to hand.

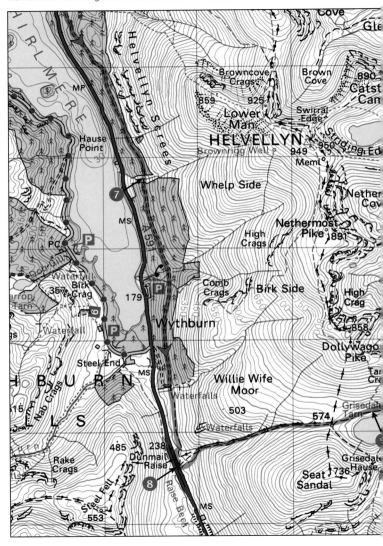

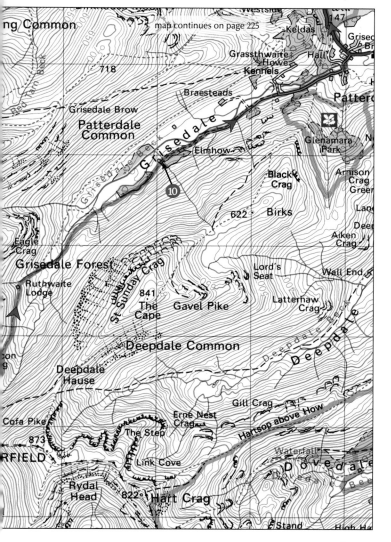

map continues on page 225

(4) As you start to descend, the path is very runnable and curves R to reach a sheepfold above the intake wall next to Stanch Gill. Here the path steepens, and is very slippery when wet, as you follow the wall line straight down the hillside towards **Legburthwaite**.

(5) Before crossing the wall, turn L off the bridleway and follow the footpath S to contour across the hillside above the wall line. After 600m cross **Fisherplace Gill**, and at the corner of the wall 350m ahead keep running SA, ignoring the tracks ascending to your L and descending to the R. Keep contouring until you reach another wall, where the path starts descending towards Helvellyn Gill. Here, turn R at a corner of the wall and follow the path over a footbridge and into the **car park**.

(6) At the S edge of the car park is a permitted path along the wide forestry track into Thirlmere woods. This climbs gently to 290m, and after 1.2km from the car park it contours away from the large track. Run along this for 900m to reach another beck, which you cross to reach another wider track on the far bank. Below you next to the lake is the water intake for the 96-mile aqueduct that supplies drinking water to Manchester.

(7) Run along the forest track and after 1km cross Whelpside Gill, then 1.3km after that the forestry track doubles back on itself and the footpath crosses

▶ **Running on the Thirlmere forestry track**

Birkside Gill on the edge of the forest and traverses the hillside alongside the wall to reach **Dunmail Raise**.

8 Here, you turn sharp L and ascend the path steeply alongside Raise Beck. There are a few rocky steps to negotiate, but eventually the gradient eases and you arrive at the pass at 574m. Ahead lies **Grisedale Tarn**; turn it to the L to intersect with the pitched path descending from Dollywaggon Pike.

Runners on the Raise Beck path

9 Run SA and down the path into Grisedale, where you join the Coast-to-Coast path. Traverse below Tarn and Falcon Crags and pass the climbing hut after Spout Crag. Use the footbridges below the hut to cross to the R bank of Grisedale Beck, and follow the bridleway down into the valley floor.

10 The track becomes a farm road; follow this all the way down **Grisedale** to emerge on the A592 next to the bridge. Turn L and follow the road for 1km to cross Glenridding Beck, then turn L again onto the Greenside road in **Glenridding** and run up the road to the pub where you started.

Surviving the winter

If you're running this route in winter, it's worth taking a survival bag rather than a flimsy foil blanket. Bags are more resilient in challenging conditions, and are key safety kit. If there's snow or ice on the fells, consider carrying a blizzard bag, as these are even more efficient at reflecting and retaining body heat in an emergency. Small lightweight down jackets that pack up into their own stuff pockets can also be a lifesaver in winter conditions.

Route 40
Pinnacle Ridge skyrunning

Start/Finish	White Lion pub, Patterdale
Distance	9.9km (6¼ miles)
Ascent/Descent	705m (2315ft)
Grade	Sky running, Level 5
Time	2hr
High point	St Sunday Crag (841m/2759ft)
Maps	1:25,000 OS Map OL5, 1:40,000 Harvey Lake District
Public transport	Bus 508 from Windermere/Penrith
Parking	Ask in pub to use their car park, or there are a few spaces in the layby next to the A592.
Warning	This is mountaineering terrain and should only be undertaken by experienced skyrunners and scramblers

The final route in this guidebook offers runners the opportunity to follow the most technical section of the Lakes Sky Ultra race route up Pinnacle Ridge on St Sunday Crag. It isn't a long run, but the technical crux is a Grade 3 scramble, where many walkers elect to rope up for security. It is not a route for a novice skyrunner – try the Langdale Horseshoe (Route 12) or the Helvellyn skyline (Route 38) for more suitable introductory skyrunning terrain. This route is for experienced skyrunners and scramblers only, and you're encouraged to avoid it at weekends or bank holidays, when less experienced walking groups may be on the route.

1 Turn L out of the pub and cross the road, keeping R of the car park. Follow the track around to the R, and at the intake wall turn L to follow it to the wall crossing below Thornhow Crag, after which you descend to the Grisedale Farm track. Turn L and follow it up the valley for 1km to **Elmhow**.

2 At the end of the Elmhow plantation, go through the gate and take the footpath up the hillside to the L alongside the plantation. Ahead, follow the zig-zags up the hillside into Blind Cove, where the ground starts to level out slightly at 450m.

3. Turn R and contour along the hillside for 1km. There are several broken gullies and scree lines descending across your path; continue to the third line of scree and turn L to ascend the faint path that ascends up the scree. The start of Pinnacle Ridge is indistinct from this point, but starts to the left of the deepest gully at NY 367 138.

4. Run up the gully and on the L you'll see a gun-shaped rock, which is called the Cannon. Beyond the Cannon, climb

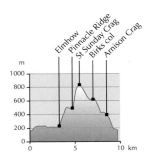

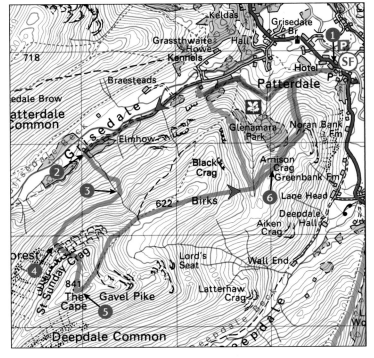

onto a ridge and follow its crest upwards. At the first large slab of rock you can keep low for an easier route. Above this there's another 50m of straightforward scrambling to reach three gendarmes (pinnacles). The technical crux of the route involves climbing the rock corner behind the pinnacles, after which the route is more exposed but technically easier. The final pinnacle can be downclimbed, and you can skirt the final buttress to veer R and reach the track leading to the top of **St Sunday Crag**. The technical difficulties can be avoided, and the most obvious escape route is gained by dropping down to the easy gully which runs parallel to the right of the ridge.

Roped scrambling on the pinnacles

5. Turn L and head NE along the ridge crest, over the head of Gavel Moss. At the col at 603m on the summit ridge of **Birks**, turn half R and head E to pick up a faint path that threads its way through the outcrops to the N of Coldcove Gill, before veering L across Trough Head and then NE along the ridgeline to **Arnison Crag**.

6. Just beyond this you'll reach the wall line, which descends to the N, past Oxford Crag and several outcrops, for 700m to reach the intake wall, where you turn R and retrace your earlier steps back to the pub in **Patterdale**.

Equip yourself for emergencies

On this, and any other, skyrunning route, it's worth carrying a couple of slings and a karabiner, so that you can make yourself safe in the event of an accident or to aid a retreat. It's safer to run with a partner and so a walker's confidence rope could also be carried – a 20m rope would be sufficient to belay a short pitch, or to do an abseil.

Appendix A
Useful contacts

Transport
Skyscanner flights search
www.skyscanner.net

Trainline for train tickets
www.thetrainline.com

National Express buses
www.nationalexpress.com

Travelline
www.traveline.info

Cumbria Council transport
www.cumbria.gov.uk
and select 'Roads & travel'

Cumbria Tourism bus information
www.golakes.co.uk/travel

Low-carbon car hire
www.co-wheels.org.uk

Accommodation

Campsites
Windermere YHA campsite
www.yha.org.uk

Low Wray campsite
www.nationaltrust.org.uk
and search for 'Low Wray'

Baysbrown Farm campsite
www.baysbrownfarmcampsite.co.uk

Great Langdale campsite
www.nationaltrust.org.uk
and search for 'Great Langdale'

Castlerigg Farm campsite
www.castlerigg.co.uk

Burns Farm campsite
www.burns-farm.co.uk

Chapel House Farm campsite
www.chapelhousefarmcampsite.co.uk

Glamping
Castlerigg Hall camping pods
www.castlerigg.co.uk

Basecamp Tipi glamping
www.basecamptipi.co.uk

Hostels
Ambleside YHA
www.yha.org.uk

Elterwater hostel
www.elterwaterhostel.co.uk

Coppermines YHA
www.yha.org.uk

Keswick YHA
www.yha.org.uk

White Horse Threldkeld bunkhouse
www.thewhitehorse-blencathra.co.uk

Accommodation finder
Cumbria Tourism
www.golakes.co.uk

Trail and fell running resources
Lakeland 50 and 100
www.lakeland100.com

Montane Trail 26
www.trail26.com

Lakes in a Day
www.lakesinaday.co.uk

Ambleside AC
www.amblesideac.co.uk

Fell Running Association (FRA)
www.fellrunner.org.uk

Icicle mountain running guiding
www.icicle-mountaineering.ltd.uk
and select 'Run'

Lake District resources
Wainwright summits map
www.walkingclub.org.uk/hills
and choose 'Wainwrights'

GPS list of Wainwrights
www.haroldstreet.org.uk/wainwrights

Free 1:25,000 OS maps
(on 3rd level of zoom)
www.streetmap.co.uk

Grizedale Forest visitor centre
www.forestry.gov.uk/grizedale

Trail and Fell Running in the Lake District

Harvey Fell Races maps 1:40,000 scale
www.harveymaps.co.uk
and look under 'UK & Ireland mapping'

Ennerdale re-wilding programme
www.wildennerdale.co.uk

Bio-security advice near water sources
www.cfinns.scrt.co.uk

Ullswater Way footpath
www.ullswater.com/the-ullswater-way/

Fix the Fells
www.fixthefells.co.uk

Friends of the Lake District
www.friendsofthelakedistrict.org.uk

MWIS weather forecast
www.mwis.org.uk/english-welsh-forecast/LD/

Met Office mountain forecast
www.metoffice.gov.uk/public/weather/
mountain-forecasts

Fell top forecast
www.lakedistrictweatherline.co.uk

Maps
Ordnance Survey
www.ordnancesurvey.co.uk

Harvey Maps
www.harveymaps.co.uk

Yellow Publications
www.yellowpublications.co.uk

Stanfords
www.stanfords.co.uk

The Map Shop
www.themapshop.co.uk

Start-point pubs
Route 1
Royal Oak, Ambleside
www.johnbarras.com

Route 2
White Lion, Ambleside
www.emberinns.co.uk
and search in 'Find your local'

Route 3
Golden Rule, Ambleside
www.goldenrule-ambleside.co.uk

Route 4
Kirkstone Inn, Kirkstone Pass
www.kirkstonepassinn.com

Route 5
Mortal Man, Troutbeck
www.themortalman.co.uk

Route 6
The Elleray, Windermere
www.elleraywindermere.com

Route 7
Tweedies Bar, Grasmere
www.dalelodgehotel.co.uk

Route 8
Eagles Head, Satterthwaite
www.eagleshead.co.uk

Route 9
Drunken Duck, Barngates
www.drunkenduckinn.co.uk

Route 10
Cuckoo Brow, Far Sawrey
www.cuckoobrow.co.uk

Route 11
Black Bull, Coniston
www.blackbullconiston.co.uk

Route 12
Old Dungeon Ghyll, Great Langdale
www.odg.co.uk

Route 13
Three Shires Inn, Little Langdale
www.threeshiresinn.co.uk

Route 14
Woolpack Inn, Hardknott
www.woolpack.co.uk

Route 15
Newfield Inn, Duddon Valley
www.newfieldinn.co.uk

Route 16
Wasdale Head Inn, Wasdale
www.wasdale.com

Route 17
The Sun, Coniston
www.thesunconiston.com

Route 18
Ship Inn, Coniston
www.robinsonsbrewery.com
and click on 'Find a pub'

Route 19
Sticklebarn pub, Langdale
www.nationaltrust.org.uk/
sticklebarn-and-the-langdales

Route 20
The Britannia pub, Elterwater
www.thebritanniainn.com

Route 21
The Fish Inn, Buttermere
www.fishinnbuttermere.co.uk

Route 22
Swinside Inn, Newlands
www.swinsideinn.com

Route 23
Fox and Hounds, Ennerdale Bridge
www.foxandhoundsinn.org

Route 24
Wasdale Head Inn, Wasdale
www.wasdale.com

Route 25
Kirkstile Inn, Loweswater
www.kirkstile.com

Route 26
Royal Oak, Braithwaite
www.royaloak-braithwaite.co.uk

Route 27
Bridge Hotel Inn, Buttermere
www.bridge-hotel.com/bridge-inn/

Route 28
Scafell Hotel pub, Rosthwaite
www.scafell.co.uk

Route 29
Dog & Gun pub, Keswick
www.thedogandgunkeswick.co.uk

Route 30
The Sun Inn, Bassenthwaite
www.suninnlakes.co.uk

Route 31
Horse & Farrier, Threlkeld
www.horseandfarrier.com

Route 32
The Royal Hotel pub, Dockray
www.the-royal-dockray.co.uk

Route 33
Brackenrigg Inn, Watermillock
www.brackenrigginn.co.uk

Route 34
Punchbowl Inn, Askham
www.punchbowlinnaskham.com

Route 35
Howtown Hotel, Howtown
www.howtown-hotel.co.uk

Route 36
Inn on the Lake, Glenridding
www.lakedistricthotels.net

Route 37
Brotherswater Inn, Sykeside
www.sykeside.co.uk/inn.php

Route 38
White Lion Inn, Patterdale
www.the-whitelion.com

Route 39
The Traveller's Rest pub, Glenridding
www.hesketbrewery.co.uk
and click on 'outlets'

Route 40
White Lion Inn, Patterdale
www.the-whitelion.com

Fell runners near Lily Tarn, Loughrigg

download the route
in GPX Format

All the routes in this guide are available for download from:

www.cicerone.co.uk/880/GPX

as GPX files. You should be able to load them into most formats of mobile device, whether GPS or smartphone.

When you go to this link, you will be asked for your email address and where you purchased the guide, and have the option to subscribe to the Cicerone e-newsletter.

Listing of Cicerone guides

For full information on all our
guides, books and eBooks,
visit our website:
www.cicerone.co.uk

Walking – Trekking – Mountaineering – Climbing – Cycling

Over 40 years, Cicerone have built up an outstanding collection of over 300 guides, inspiring all sorts of amazing adventures.

Every guide comes from extensive exploration and research by our expert authors, all with a passion for their subjects. They are frequently praised, endorsed and used by clubs, instructors and outdoor organisations.

All our titles can now be bought as **e-books**, **ePubs** and **Kindle** files and we also have an online magazine – **Cicerone Extra** – with features to help cyclists, climbers, walkers and trekkers choose their next adventure, at home or abroad.

Our website shows any **new information** we've had in since a book was published. Please do let us know if you find anything has changed, so that we can publish the latest details. On our **website** you'll also find great ideas and lots of detailed information about what's inside every guide and you can buy **individual routes** from many of them online.

It's easy to keep in touch with what's going on at Cicerone by getting our monthly **free e-newsletter**, which is full of offers, competitions, up-to-date information and topical articles. You can subscribe on our home page and also follow us on **Facebook** and **Twitter** or dip into our **blog**.

Cicerone – the very best guides for exploring the world.

CICERONE

2 Police Square Milnthorpe Cumbria LA7 7PY
Tel: 015395 62069 info@cicerone.co.uk
www.cicerone.co.uk and **www.cicerone-extra.com**